Great White Shark Tales

By James A Calderwood

In Memory of John Henry Ives

Revised Edition   2018

All rights reserved. No part of this book may be reproduced or transmitted in any form or by any means, electronic or mechanical, including photocopying, recording, or by any information storage and retrieval system, without permission in writing from the copyright owner.

Great White shark sinks fishing boat

The sun was shining, and there was a light breeze blowing. The snapper fish were running. All of this was a good combination for a good day's fishing.

I drove my old utility down to the jetty, then unloaded the fishing tackle bag and my lunch box; I then walked down the jetty to the mooring line. I had a small tender dinghy tied on a running lead.   As I pulled the dinghy in, I noticed that most of the other professional fishermen had already left for the fishing grounds; I climbed down to the dinghy, then stowed my gear. I untied the dinghy; then I started to row out to my twenty-one-foot timber fishing boat.

When I arrived, I tied the painter rope to the side of the boat, then tossed the bags, then climbed over the side. I fiddled around checking the motor and then started the Blaxland pup motor by hand by pulling the flywheel over compression. The dinghy painter rope was tied to the mooring line near the buoy; I then cast off ready to head out to the fishing grounds.

The motor went pop, pop, pop as I put it into gear and headed off out through the harbor entrance. I was looking forward to the days fishing, as the weather had been quite windy for the last few days, and I had not been able to go out.

The boat had a mast and sail, which I seldom used; this sail was mainly for emergencies. There was a small cabin; behind this was a sizeable wet well to hold the fish. This well had round holes through the boat's bottom to allow fresh water to circulate to keep the fish alive.   As I arrived at my best snapper fishing spot, I noticed that another fisherman was already fishing. It was a friend of mine. I stopped the motor, tossed the anchor out, and tied it off the cathead. I was about forty meters away from my mate.

I got my heavy line out of the fishing tackle box, then I put some bait on the large hooks and dropped it into the water. In a short time, I had my first large snapper. A few minutes later, I had about fifteen large snappers flapping about in the well of the boat.

I was pulling one more towards the boat when the line went slack. I pulled a snapper head into the boat. I had company as the head had been nipped off by a shark.

I stood up and looked around the boat and noticed a large dark shape moving through the water. The shark came closer to the boat and started to circle it. It was attracted by the noise of the snapper thrashing around. I was a bit angry because the fishing had been excellent up to now.

I watched as the shark swam past my boat and did a rough reckoning of its length compared to my boat. This shark must have been about eighteen feet long.

The shark bumped the boat's bottom, nearly knocking me off my feet. I decided to pull up the anchor and move to another spot. Suddenly there was an almighty heave under the boat as the shark had charged the bottom of my boat. Two of the planks in the boat's bottom caved in, and water came pouring into the boat. I was in trouble; the boat was sinking, and the shark was still circling.

The boat was sinking quickly. I yelled to my mate, who had been watching the shark circle my boat. He rushed and started his motor, then ran to cast off the anchor rope into the water; he swung the nose of the boat around and headed for me. I was standing on the top of my cabin, watching as the transom of my boat was starting to go under the water. My mate's boat arrived as my boat was disappearing under the waves, I was climbing the mast. I did not want to be fish food. The bow of my mate's boat came across the side of the sinking boat; I jumped across and landed on the deck of his boat.

We watched the shark circle and ate most of the half-stunned snapper, which was floating where my boat had sunk. My lunch box was about the only thing which floated off my boat. The rest has gone to the bottom. My mate had lost his anchor. If he had tried to pull it up, I would have been history.

As we traveled back to the jetty, I commented that I would have two lives. The one before the shark sank my boat and the other starting now. If he had not been at the same fishing spot, I surely would have been shark food.

A near Catastrophe

I had a phone call from a friend inviting me to go on a deep-sea fishing trip with him on his large yacht. A tuna farm operator he was friends with had phoned him about a tuna pen they were towing back to Port Lincoln. This pen had a school of wild tuna following the large towed cage.

These fish would be transferred to a large pen with netted sides and bottom to be fed and fattened up for the lucrative sashimi market. The tuna industry had been in the doldrums before the live fish fattening program was introduced. The cost of catching the fish just to make canned tuna was not paying.

When the fish was towed behind the large ocean-going fishing boat, the towing speed had to be kept at about one and a half knots. Any faster than this would spook the captured fish, which caused a lot of mortalities among them. The towing had to keep going through all types of weather conditions. The cages could not be left. Sharks would chew their way through the netting, and then the fish would escape

The weather was very windy from the south. The forecast was for the wind to abate and the weather to remain calm for a few days.

I have often wondered how the weather forecasters ply their trade. Do they have a giant dart board with numbers on it to check the corresponding numbers the dart thrown by the blind folded man hits with a chart of the weather, or maybe they have a seer or soothsayer locked in a dark room where they consult each other? They should really have a window they could look out and see if it is raining or fair weather.

Bob and I set out for Williams Island past Cape Catastrophe to meet up with the fishing boat towing the net. The weather was not nice; we headed into a large ocean swell. The yacht dipped its nose and tossed the spray back over the dog house where we sat. We were motoring as we were driving straight at the sea and wind; the sails would have been useless.

The weather forecast was for the wind to abate and fine the next day.

Williams Island was one of a group of eight that Matthew Flinders had named as he explored and mapped the coast of South Australia many years ago.

A group of men had set out for the shore to search for water to replenish the supply on the ship the Investigator. They had all perished when a huge wave had upturned their long boat. The islands were named after these men.

We were pleased to get to Williams Island finally and to be able to shelter in a small bay on the north western side. The huge swell still sneaked around the corner of the headland, making it uncomfortable aboard the yacht.

As we sat waiting, the wind slowly started to go to the north. Now the sea was tumbling into where we were trying to shelter. We started the motor and headed for West Bay, which was about a kilometer to the north. The sea was a lot flatter in West Bay. We had a bottle of red wine and some cheese sandwiches and then went to bed.

The yacht was leaning over and rolling madly. The wind in the rigging was howling like a banshee. Bob yelled for me to come upside and help steer the yacht as we were drifting. The anchor was not holding against the bullet winds that rolled down the steep hills we had anchored in the lee of. We drifted about four times that night in the terrible wind. About three in the morning, the wind started to abate somewhat. We finally got some sleep.

In the morning, the wind was from the west, quite strong, but nowhere as bad as during the night. We could see smoke rising from the exhaust of the large fishing boat towing the tuna cage in the distance.

Bob decided that the weather had settled enough for us to venture out to see if we could catch some tuna. The headland of the bay was sheltering us from the swell. As we drove out from West Point, the sea was very rough. The waves were peaking and were about four meters high; the tide and the wind had caused a nasty joggle sea. The yacht would be lifted atop one of these ugly waves then the wave would drop out from under us.

A dinghy was in a cradle on the stern of the yacht, some of the ropes had become loose, and the dinghy was sliding around. Bob had a lot of safety lines tied into the rigging for occasions like these. Bob clambered past me on his way to secure the errant dinghy. A huge wave hit the side of the yacht, and he grabbed for a safety rope; the end had been untied, he was toppling over the rail of the yacht. Quick as a flash, I grabbed his belt and collar of the heavy jacket he was wearing; I rolled over to get a lot of purchase and pulled him back over the rail into the cockpit. Bob did not mention this incident. I did a lot of thinking as to what I would have been able to do if he had fallen overboard into the sea. The yacht was surfing down the waves and slipping sideways off others. We had no ladder on the stern to allow a person to climb back aboard.

I was on a fishing trip with Bob many years later in the same area in a similar sea. Bob asked me if I remembered the day he had nearly gone overboard. He said that he thought that would have been the end of his life. He would have drowned. I did agree with his theory as I did not know if I could have picked him up.

Shark cage movies

I was working on a sardine netting boat, and after a hard night's work with the heavy nets, I was ready for a good sleep before the next night working on the nets again when it got dark.

We pulled into a sheltered bay on Neptune Island, ready for a good kip. There were two other boats there already.

One of the boats was a restored ketch that was used for charter work. I could see some people on board filming and a winch with a shark diving cage suspended from it. A guy was chumming the water with a burley to attract sharks. I scanned the sea around the ketch and noticed the fins of some large white pointer sharks swimming around. After looking for a while and noting the different markings and sizes of the sharks, there seemed to be six or seven sharks present. A guy on the ketch was tossing a half tuna out, and the sharks were jostling to get it as it was quickly towed back toward the boat. Another two guys were filming the antics of the sharks. This was not a tourist charter; all of the equipment looked too large and expensive for this. One of the organizers looked familiar; it was one of Australia's White Pointer shark experts. He had been a shark attack victim himself.   The filming of the Pointers attacking the various pieces of tuna was being wrapped up; I watched a guy climb into the shark cage ready to be winched down into the water; he had a large camera and some undersea lighting.

The winch lowered the cage into the water. I had surmised by this time that most of the crew were Americans. The shark cage was almost level with the water when one of the film crew climbed across and stood on top of the shark cage; he had a large movie camera with him.

I thought that this was a pretty stupid thing to do but kept watching as the cage finally submerged to about a meter under the water. The cameraman was almost to his waist in the water, without the protection of the shark cage.

From where I was standing on the sardine boat, I could see all around the cage and out to sea. All of the film crew watched the guys with the cage and filmed them attentively. There was not a shark lookout, which I thought was pretty stupid.

I noticed a wake from a speeding shark coming toward the cage; I yelled, "Get out of the water "the guy said, "it's ok, buddy. We have been feeding them," I yelled "look behind you! " He turned and saw the large shark heading toward him. The guy dropped the camera and heaved himself up the cable holding the cage. The large White Pointer shot straight over the top of the cage, just missing the camera man, I yelled

"evidently, that one was still hungry. "

Great White Toothache

My brother Peter and I had walked the three miles home from school. It had been a pretty hot day in our one-teacher school.

When we had arrived home, uncle George was visiting; he was sitting on the veranda talking to dad. Both of the men had a bottle of beer each, and by the look of the pile of bottles, they had been at it for a while.

Uncle George lived on a property that bordered the coastline. He had a lot of horses and had won a few big races with them. Peter and I always used to like listening to the stories that he and dad told. The stories always used to get better as they drank some beer.

Uncle George had been down to the rough coastline and had noticed a big school of salmon lying in the shallows in the first bay. He suggested to dad that we all go down to the beach and toss a plug of Gelignite into the school of fish.

Most of the properties in the area had a case of Gelignite. This was used to help dig some post holes in the limestone rock and was also used to help deepen some of the wells when the water level dropped.

Uncle George left in his utility. We were to meet him at the beach at five-thirty in the afternoon, ready for the big adventure. Both Peter and I were pretty keyed up about this adventure as we did not get out too much usually.

As we drove down to the beach, we could see the large school of salmon lying in the shallows along the shoreline of the beach. Uncle George and Cousin Anthony were waiting on the beach. They had carried down a basket and some wheat bags. We were carrying some bags; dad had a sugar bag with a flagon of port wine, which was always used to warm up with after being in the water collecting the fish. Of course, we kids did not use this.

Uncle George got a plug of Gelignite out of a kitbag, which was in the fishing basket. He fitted the detonator and short fuse, he walked to the water's edge then got a box of matches out, he took a match and held it on the end of the short fuse the struck the box along the top of it. The fuse spluttered to life; Uncle George had a bit of a run-up, like a cricketer, and bowled the gelignite out among the salmon. Whoomph, a huge spray of water erupted amongst the fish.

As the water subsided, the salmon were floating on top of the water in a stunned state; we all waded into the water and carried and tossed the stunned fish out, high on the sand to be bagged later. Dad yelled to Uncle George and pointed behind him; George turned and saw a large fin cutting through the water toward him. We all scrambled out of the water.

We stood on the shore watching a huge white shark speeding through the water, gobbling our fish up. Dad suggested that we collect the fish close to shore; just after this, the shark almost beached itself, as it picked up a few salmon in its lunge forward.

We were loading the few fish we had tossed on the beach into the bags and baskets when George came down to the water line with a plug of gelignite and a large salmon. He already had the fuse and detonator in the plug. George cut the salmon with his pocket knife, so it was bleeding; he then poked the plug down the salmon's neck and lit the fuse.

The fish lobbed right in front of the enormous shark, which opened its mouth, swallowed the fish, and swam on. In about ten seconds, the gelignite exploded. The water was filled with the red blood of the giant shark. Pieces of the shark's head were landing on the beach around us. Peter and I picked up some of the huge sharp teeth.

The fish gathering was resumed; some of the salmon were waking from their stunned state and were swimming off. The shark carcass was on the beach, as the tide was receding still.

Before we started to carry the fish up the beach to load on the utilities, George put one foot after another to measure the headless shark; the body of the shark was close to thirteen feet long without its head. The shark must have been about sixteen feet long.

Henrys Christmas Turkey

Henry was a fascinating man. He owned a large property about six miles away from where we lived. His son was living alone on this property after his marriage broke up some years before.

Henry was one to like a tipple. In most sheds, there were a bottle or two of whisky or port wine secreted away in case medication was needed. The property was a large, prosperous sheep station of about twenty-five thousand acres, which ran four thousand sheep and about one hundred and fifty cattle on a reedy swamp area. The property adjoined the rugged coastline, which had a small sandy beach at one end.

I was going through this property one day to get to the beach; there was usually good fishing on a low cliff just before the beach area. I called at the house to let Don, Henry's son that I was going through their property to the beach fishing.

When I knocked on the door of the house, Henry came out to meet me.

Henry was in his early seventies and was a really good yarn spinner.

"Is Don home?" "No, Don has gone away for a few weeks. I am here by myself looking after the property.

It was a pleasant sunny day, as it had been for a few days, which was quite rare, as the area along this coastline was always known for its wind. 'Good windmill country' was called by the locals.

Most properties had windmills to pump water situated in most of the large paddocks, as there was excellent water at a shallow depth. Most of the windmills had a stone tank and a sheep trough made out of the local limestone.

Henry commented on the calm weather and asked me if I would like to have him come with me fishing.

I was really pleased with this idea. Henry went to the shed and got his fishing rod and two long fish spears. He also had a bag out of the fridge with a couple of rabbits that he had shot; these were used to feed the three sheep dogs.

"This should be good weather for crayfish!" Henry explained when he took the spears from the corner of the car shed. He then took two bottles of beer from the fridge and placed them in the bag with the cold rabbits. We were talking as we drove across to the beach. "I don't think I will be using any of the crayfish spots anymore; I think I am getting past climbing down the cliffs to get to them. Don doesn't eat them; I will show you where I've been catching crayfish since I was a kid." I was pretty pleased to hear about this as crayfish was a real delicacy. " Thank you very much, Henry." I said as we drove through the large paddock.

Near the road leading to the beach, there was a large she-oak tree. A large wedge-tailed eagle was perched in the tree. The eagle would have had a two-meter wing span. The large bird flew away as we approached the tree. "Did I ever tell you about my wedge-tail eagle story? "   This was what I really liked about people like Henry and my father-in-law John Henry. There was always a hint of a tale to be told about most things. It just needed a catalyst to eke it out of their memory.

A man Henry knew had driven up to stay for a few days, some years ago. He was not the kind of person one would ever think of as a mate.

He never bought and booze or provisions and usually expected to go home with a few fish, some crayfish, and a couple of dressed ducks or chickens.

"The guy's name was Bert, a bit of a moocher. I could almost predict when he would appear. One special time he always came to stay was just before Christmas. This was evidently a good time for Bert to stock up on

Christmas poultry and fish to feed his family."

For some reason, the lambing percentages on the property were low one year. I had separated the ewes which did not have a lamb and had mated them to lamb in November.

One problem was that there was a large population of these wedge-tail eagles in the district. One of their favorite foods was newborn lambs. I have seen the birds working as a pair swooping on a ewe with the new lamb. As the ewe would chase one of these big birds away, the other would come in at a different angle and grab the lamb with its long sharp claws and fly off.

"In the normal lambing period in late April, there were all of the other properties lambing at the same time; this evened things out as far as lost lambs were concerned. I was dealing with about fifty eagles." Henry took out a tin of Champion Ready Rubbed tobacco and rolled a cigarette. He lit it then continued the story.

"I went to check the sheep one morning and found a dead ewe, which had evidently died trying to give birth. A mob of about ten eagles was on the ground, squabbling over the carcass. I went home and found five rabbit traps. I took them back and set them around the dead ewe. I had some extra-long stakes to pin the traps down with, so the eagle would not fly away with the trap on its foot."

He butted his cigarette in the ashtray of the four-wheel-drive International utility.

"The next morning, I went to check the traps and had found five birds flopping around trying to take off. I noticed that there were no other eagles perched on trees as there usually were. They had been frightened off by the antics of the captured birds."

Henry took a bottle of beer out of the bag; he then found his pocket knife in his pocket. He opened the small blade then removed the bottle cap. He handed the bottle to me for the first drink.

"I dispatched all of the birds with a shot to the head with my .22 rifle. When I did this, I had a bright idea. One of my bright ideas was to tie two of the birds to each of the large she-oaks the eagles usually perched on and let them swing in the wind; I had some binder twine with me. I parked the ute under a branch the tossed the birds onto the tray; I tied the twine around the legs of the birds, then climbed up and hung them on the tree branch. Two of the others were left on the ground near the dead ewe as a warning. The largest I took home."

We had arrived at the gate which led into the paddock, which had the cliffs and small beach adjoining it. Henry went to open the gate. I drove through, he shut the gate, then got in to finish the story. He had a long swig on the beer bottle when back in the utility.

"When I arrived home, I filled a large kettle with water and put it on the wood stove to boil, as I was waiting for the kettle, the missus came into the kitchen, she wanted to know what I was doing. I said you would see later".

The beer bottle was passed back to him. He drained the last drop. "I cut the head, legs, and the ends of the long wings off the eagle; I put the eagle in the tub which was used for scalding poultry and wild ducks to loosen their feathers to pluck them."

We had arrived at the fishing spot on the low cliffs. I stopped the ute. "I poured the hot water over the Eagle, and it really stank as the hot water had seeped into the feathers. Chickens and ducks do not smell very nice after the scalding water treatment. The eagle smell was a different ball game. I removed the guts. The insides of the eagle smelled worse as they ate a lot of carrion. I persevered with the job and then hooked the legs in the rear hole, which had been cut to remove the gut.

The finished product did look a bit like a turkey but not as big. I wrapped it with grease-proof paper and then a layer of newspaper and placed it in the large kerosene operated freezer in the shed." We started to take our fishing gear out of the utility.

"A week later, Bert turned up for his free Christmas poultry, crayfish, and fish supplies. We netted a nice haul of fish from a set net off the beach. While waiting for the fish to mesh in the net, we drank a flagon of my Port wine. There were a few nice crayfish caught one still day. There was no other poultry sent to the chopping block to have their heads removed, though." As we walked to the edge of the cliff with our tackle, Henry continued the tale.

"Bert had commented on how good some of the ducks looked. This all fell on deaf ears as far as I was concerned. I could see Bert was a bit worried he was going to miss out."

The top was removed from the last beer bottle in case it was to get warm in the sun. We had a mouth full each. He continued.

"The large freezer had some containers of ice in it. As Bert was filling the ice box in the boot of his car and placing a nice lot of fish and the crayfish ready for the trip home, I pulled my small Turkey out of the freezer and gave it to Bert. I had told him that it had been a sickly runt and had not grown as big as the other birds. Bert had never been offered one of the many turkeys which lived around our sheds before and was very thankful. He tossed his suitcase into the car, thanked me, and The missus then shot through back home."

We baited the hooks and cast the lines into the water. "The wife and I had a bit of a chuckle as Bert drove off.

I noticed that Bert had missed two of his normal mooching visits; this did not really worry us. The wife and I had driven to town for business and were walking down the street when we saw Bert walking along the street toward us. As we met, we had a bit of a chat; the subject of the runt turkey had entered the conversation. Bert's wife had put the turkey on the stove in a big baking dish with a lid. He said the kitchen had not smelt very nice at all. In the true form of a moocher, Bert and his family had tried to eat the eagle but had to give up when they could not cut or chew the meat. Bert had taken the eagle to the large dog. The dog would not eat the bird."

I caught a nice Trevally; Henry also caught one. We unhooked them and put them into the bag. We were both laughing at the story.

"As Bert wandered off down the street, we had a really good laugh amongst ourselves. I had resisted the urge to tell Bert where his Christmas meal had really come from."

The day exploring Henry's favorite fishing spots had been very rewarding, with good company, good fishing and four nice crayfish to share. Plus, there were some more stories to share.

PS

Retelling these stories brings a feeling of the story returning as if it were yesterday. This was told to me forty-five years ago. Henry died about three years after this.

The Shark Wranglers

We are looking for a good worker to do a job – what a good job description. Count me out. This job description outlined duties that needed to be performed.

1 To be able to travel in a small overloaded boat in rough weather in the Southern Ocean. 2 to be willing to enter a cage towing tuna and catch large sharks and evict them from the cage. 3 Be prepared to mend torn nets. 5. Do not hurt the sharks if possible.

During the Tuna season in South Australia, a fleet of boats venture out into the Southern Ocean to net schools of Tuna. When the tuna is caught in the purse seine net, another boat tows as a floating cage to the net. The purse seine net is opened and joined to the towing cage. A hole is opened in the cage. The tuna fish is hunted into the cage supported by a thick polythene circular tube of about forty meters across. The holes for transfer are then closed up.

When the tuna fills the cage, it is closed. It is then towed at about one and a half knots, very slow as not to spook the tuna and have them panic and charge the sides of the net. Towing this large fish-filled net takes a lot of power and, therefore, fuel to bring it back to the feeding grounds just out of Port Lincoln, South Australia.

If really rough weather hits, many of the shackles holding the cage to the floating ring get stretched and need replacing. The operators have to endure a trip in a five-meter open boat to the ring, which is far astern from the towing boat, to do the repairs. This is extreme work in about as tough a condition as a most extreme job. Sharks abound in these waters. There are many species. All are looking for an easy meal. There are Whaler sharks, Grey Nurse sharks, Mako Sharks, Hammer Head Sharks, Tiger Sharks, and Great White sharks. They all have the ability to chew holes in the tough netting of the cage with their sharp serrated teeth.

The caged Tuna must seem like a bonus to them — a Supermarket on the ocean.

When a shark is found in the cage, it is imperative to evict this animal and close the hole it has made. If the tuna were to find a large hole, they may all escape in-masse, following the leader. This would be a disaster for the hard-working fisherman.

The tuna circle around in the cage as they are being towed. This creates a vortex that has the tendency to suck the divers to the bottom of the cage, making working there exhausting hard work.

When a shark is found in the cage, a diver has to spook it to tangle in the outside net then cut a hole in the net to eject it out. This is very dangerous work. Some sharks are more easily spooked than others and often turn and try to bite the diver.

After the shark is tossed out, the diver then has to sew up the holes found in the net. Do I hear any volunteers for the job? I have my hands deep in my pockets.

When cages are moored in place out from Port Lincoln, the shark problem is still there. The divers have to dive into the cage, remove any dead fish, and check for unwanted intruders and mend holes. Some of the large sharks have been known to have been shot with a Power head with a shotgun shell in it, before being lifted over the side of the cage with the winch on the feed boat. This is not allowed now

The feed boats feed the Tuna on locally caught Pilchards, a type of sardine. Boats travel to the farms in all weather conditions to do this almost every day. The tuna is fattened for the lucrative Sashimi markets in Asia.

The hey-days of this industry have passed as many other countries with cheap labor are now farm fattening fish. Many different fish are now farmed this way. Port Lincoln has many Kingfish farms. The kingfish are bred in a hatchery, and when certain, they are a certain size transferred to the farm pens.

Malcolm and the shark

We had finished our small harvest on the farm at Sheringa. As usual, the kangaroos and emus had reaped the major portion of the crop. I had tried to bolster the fences up higher and also shoot a few of the emus to frighten them off the crops. We could not get near the mongrels.

The emu population in the neighboring grazing property was very large; even with the fences built up, the emus would circle the boundary of the seven-hundred-acre block and find a way in from a different paddock. When the mob of about forty emus was grazing the crop, there was always a look out on top of a high hill. I rarely got within a mile of the mob of wreckers. There were large areas of the crop dug up into piles where the emus lay when they were not eating the barley crop.

There were Learn to swim classes at the beach at Elliston, some forty kilometers away, so we rented an old bond wood caravan at the Elliston Caravan Park. The kids could go swimming and see their school friends, and I could try my new purchase out. I had bought an old runabout boat from one of Glenys's cousins in Port Lincoln.

The water temperature in Elliston was very cold as the deep ocean was very close. All of the mothers would take the kids down to the beach and then coax the poor children into the icy water while they sat on the beach rugged up with a heavy coat on most days.

We had been doing a bit of fishing in the afternoons; when the kids had finished the swimming lessons and had found a few places where we caught some really nice sized King George whiting, we would fillet the fish, then I would take the fillets to a friend's shop where he would freeze them.

We would take them back to the farm when we went to check the windmills to see if they were pumping water and check the sheep, dogs, and chickens.

One of the other guys in the caravan park was a farmer from about sixty kilometers away whose father owned a large island called Flinders Island. Malcolm always showed off his biggest fish, as did I. Malcolm owned a large boat with a hundred horse power motor on it. He would go out to the island to help his father and then catch some of the very large whitings which lived around the island.

One evening Malcolm walked over with a moderate-sized snapper and had a bit of brag as to how he had found the spot and how no one else knew about this area. I had done a bit of work with some of the abalone divers, shelling the abalone and driving the boat when they were under water. One of the guys had said about the snapper fishing and how there was only one place where they had seen snapper close to the coast. I told Malcolm that I would see him the next day out on the water.

We were all in the friend's shop when one of the school teachers walked in and started to talk about fishing. I asked Danny whether he would like to come out to try to catch a snapper. Danny was pretty keen on this idea, so we made time after lunch the next day to have a trip. We had to go to the farm to feed the dogs and do the normal check on everything else.

I met up with Danny, and we launched the boat at Anxious Bay and then headed out to where I thought that Malcolm and his wife Pam would be. We were not disappointed as the boat was exactly where the divers had said the snapper lived. It was a reasonably still day, and the sea was quite flat, which was a bonus in the Elliston area, as there was usually a strong sea breeze every afternoon.

We parked about thirty meters away from Malcolm and Pam and tossed our heavy fishing lines into the water. Malcolm yelled to us, then pulled a nice snapper out of the water. It would have weighed about three kilograms.

Danny caught a fish of about the same size. I then noticed that Malcolm had a tussle on his hands as he had caught a big fish; he was playing with this fish trying to tire it so he could pull it into the boat. Finally, he pulled the snapper into the boat; he then held it up to show it off. This was a nice fish. It would weigh in at about six kilograms.

Pam started to point behind him and waved her arms. Malcolm said, "What the hell is wrong with you Pam," he turned around and saw a huge white pointer shark slowly subsiding back into the water

. The shark's body had been about two meters out of the water and was slipping back. Malcolm got an enormous fright, as did we. I had never seen a large white pointer close and had no idea as to the breadth and depth of the body of these creatures. This shark was about the same girth as a large fat bull

The shark game and lay next to Malcolm's boat, which was over five meters long and looked about the same length. I told Danny to wind his line in, and if he caught a fish to toss the line overboard as I reckoned the shark was longer than our boat, I was madly winding my line at the same time. The fin of the shark was above the transom of Malcolm's boat, with about a quarter of the shark's body out of the water. One big black eye was out of the water, looking straight toward us.

Malcolm started the motor on his boat, as did we; he then gunned the motor and shot past the shark as he quickly pulled the anchor up. The large shark rolled over and over in the water from the turbulence from the propeller. I pulled the anchor and headed in toward the shore.

It was a lot rougher inshore as there was a back wash from the reef bottom, but Danny and I did not want the shark following us.

Malcolm was back at the boat ramp loading his boat when we finally

got back to shore, Glenys and the kids were waiting there also.

Poor Pam lost her voice for two days after the fright she had from the unwelcome visitor. I certainly neither didn't want to go snapper fishing again for a while.

There was a large wooden prawn trawler which quite often parked in a small sheltered bay on Waldegrave Island to shelter from the night's prawn trawling in the area. We had seen this boat on numerous occasions when we were out fishing and often wondered why they had a large pink buoy about twenty meters behind the boat. Three days later, they caught this shark. It was fifteen foot six inches in the old measure long.

Evidently, a few people had been hassled by this shark. One was a semiprofessional fisherman who noticed that the stern of his boat was getting lower in the water.

He thought that he may have forgotten to put the plugs in the boat, and the water was coming in. He went to the stern of the eighteen-foot boat and noticed the large shark laying on its back with the bottom of the outboard motor and propeller in its mouth.

Don started the motor with the throttle forward to get some revs without having the motor in gear. The shark got a stomach full of exhaust fumes and floated for a while, farting copious amounts of bubbles from its rear before it could get rid of the extra buoyancy. Another guy was in the shallows in a two-meter tinny dinghy. This shark really rattled his nerves.

We had seen large sharks swimming at Sheringa as we had gone salmon fishing; there were some high cliffs which one had to drive along to get to the surf beach where the salmon was. It was a lot different to see one close-up.

Louie's large wood pile

Louie had left the farm and moved to town. His health was failing. His wife had died five years ago.

The farm work was too much for his seventy-five years.

Louie's son Tom took the farm over and worked hard to finish clearing the good land on the farm. Tom would call to Port Lincoln and pay me a visit. He would have his wife June and the three kids, Little Louie, Sally, and Vera.

Tom always bought a load of logs and stumps on the utility truck. These stumps were very appreciated as all of the home relied on the stumps for hot water, cooking and also kept the house warm in winter, being used in the old fireplace in the lounge room.

Louie noticed one day that some of the smaller pieces of wood he had kept aside to use in the Metters stove in the kitchen, which also heated the water for washing and bathing, had been stolen. Louie kept watch and left certain logs and stumps; these disappeared over time. Some crook was stealing his firewood.

The rear of the house block was only fenced with a low mesh fence with a topping of one strand of plain fence wire. Louie did notice some woman's shoe prints leading to the wood heap when the soil was damp and soft from the night's rain.

Aha, Louie had found who the wood thief was, Miss Murphy, an old maid next door. He climbed over the fence then walked to the back door of the house. He knocked loudly.

Miss Murphy answered the door. "I have been losing fire wood from my wood pile and have seen tracks leading from the fence to my wood heap."

Miss Murphy looked at Louie with a nasty stare." I will get the police to you. You old mongrel. The only time I have been into your yard was to get my pussy cat from your wood pile."

Louie thought that this might stop the firewood from disappearing from the heap. He was wrong. The tracks still crossed the fence. Louie was not to be beaten.

Tom and his family came to visit one weekend. "Could you please bring me a small jam-jar filled with some of the blasting powder we use to split the gum logs with"? Tom agreed to do so but was wondering what his father wanted the explosives for." Did you want some fuse?" "No, she'll be right, just the gun powder." Tom realized he was not going to find out what this was going to be used for.

The next day Louie noticed that Miss Murphy was walking to the shops. Louie went to the back shed and took a brace, and bit to the wood pile. He selected a small stump the size Miss Murphy had taken a shine to. A hole was bored deep into the middle of the stump. Some black powder was poured into the hole. Louie then hammered a piece of round wood into this hole.

The wood pile was checked regularly to see if the doctored stump had been stolen. After three weeks, Louie was disappointed to see that it was left behind; firewood was still being taken.

One morning, while collecting some morning's wood to start the fire, he noticed that the doctored stump had been taken.

Two days later, all hell broke loose. A muffled bang came from Miss Murphy's house. The back door opened, and Miss Murphy came running out. A cloud of smoke followed her. "You rotten mongrel Louie you have tried to kill me. You have tried to blow me up with a bomb". "How would I do that." "You must have put something in one of your stumps " 'How would you get one of my stumps in your stove." Miss Murphy thought for a while. "I am going to go and get the Police" Louie smiled and answered. "So, you have been stealing my fire wood you old crook." Miss Murphy turned and let out a vindictive string of oaths, then reentered her house.

Evidently, Miss Murphy had to get a new front door for the fire box on the stove. The old one had been snapped in half from the explosion.

Abalone diving problems

We had gone to Elliston after harvest on the farm so the kids could go to a Learn to swim program run by the Education department. We stayed in one of our neighbor's shack on the shore of Waterloo Bay. The shack was built out of the local redgum timber and had warped over the years, making it a bit unstable in a strong wind. The shack was up on poles to give a great view of the bay. As one walked up the side steps, the shack would move in time.

A friend of ours who had a shop at Elliston was also a fish buyer. He dealt mainly in Cray Fish and Abalone. Most other fish were either caught and eaten by locals or sold by the two local fishermen to the hotel and a couple of shops.

Some of the Abalone divers had their families living nearby in the shack area. We got to know some of them very well.

They were a mixed lot. One man had been a school teacher, another a farmer, one an insurance agent, another a sheep shearer — even a lawyer dove for the elusive succulent. I always presumed the lawyer was in a good profession as he would have been immune to being eaten by a shark.

The main place the guys dove for Abalone was thirty kilometers offshore, an Island called Flinders Island.

The strong winds in the area usually dictated whether they traveled out to the island. On other occasions, they worked along the cliffs and closer islands like Little and Big Waldegrave Island,

I worked for four different guys as a Sheller when we were in town. I would winch the netting bag filled with abalone up and onto the boat, then send down another net bag. The bag was helped up with a small parachute which was filled with air from the Hookah air hose. The deal was that I was to get a percentage of the catch.

When the bag was onboard, I would take the abalone from the bag and cut the meat from the shell and guts. One had to be vigilant about not running over the airline of the diving unit or getting too close to the rocks. Some nasty waves sometimes built up around the rocky headlands.

I headed out with John this day to Flinders Island, about an hour and a half trip. We started in deep water on the western side of the island. John had been working for about two hours. He had sent up three bags of abalone.

He had not been filling the fourth bag for very long when I could see him coming to the surface. He had a brown stain following him. He climbed over the side of the boat and took his mouthpiece out, and started to curse in a compelling way. Blood was pulsing from a wound on his face. He took the hood off the wetsuit; I noticed that a large piece of skin had been torn out of his cheek. I went and found the small first aid kit in the cabin of the boat.

We both went to work on the hole in his cheek to try to stop the bleeding. After a short while, we succeeded.

He was having problems with large leather jackets, A colorful fish with very strong teeth. They use the teeth to eat barnacles and other shells off the rocks by crushing their shells with their teeth. The leather jackets were extremely aggressive this day. They attacked the freshly levered off abalone and were gulping down large chunks of meat. John had been hitting at them with the abalone lever, which he used to help the abalone off the rocks. One of the leather jackets had evidently sidled up from behind John. The diving mask stopped his peripheral side vision. A small piece of skin showed through next to where the mask, hood, and regulator in his mouth, which supplied the air. The large leather jacket had bitten deeply and then spun in a circle to tear the large chunk of meat from Johns's face.

There was no chance of John diving for abalone that day or a few after the local doctor had sewn the edges of the hole together with about twenty stitches.

Flinders Island is a great home for large Great White Sharks. The sharks can smell blood from a great distance; to be swimming with a trace of blood in the water could be suicide.

Laxettes In The Caravan

I was working on a building site helping to dig the trenches for the water and septic pipes. The work was pretty hard as there was a lot of limestone rock on the block of land.

There was also a gang of carpenters putting up the framing for a new house.

The foundations had been poured some weeks before. I had laid all of the pipes through and under the foundations before the men had started. The work now was to put the copper pipes up into the walls, ready for the bathroom, laundry, and the hot water service in the ceiling.

There was an old caravan at the rear of the unfenced block and a small prefabricated toilet block. The block was owned by a young German couple who had migrated to Australia a few years before. They had saved and bought the block, and were living in the caravan until they could afford to build a house.

I had spoken to this young man and his wife as they had been getting ready to head off in the mornings to go to work. They seemed like a very nice couple. There was one large problem; they had a dog, a German Shepherd dog.

Every morning without fail, this huge dog would start to bark. The dog had been locked in the caravan for the day until the owners came home. As soon as the dog heard the push bikes arriving, he stopped barking. We all had worked out that the old caravan was acting as a sounding board like a guitar case magnifying the noise from the strings. We could not concentrate on our work. One of the guys went to the caravan and yelled at the dog; I suppose as he did not speak German, the dog did not understand him. He just barked louder. The lad working for me even tried hitting the side of the caravan with a piece of cut-off flooring board; this made a hell of a whack. The dog had shut up for about ten seconds then went berserk, barking, scratching, and snarling.

One of the carpenters had been a bit of a lad in his time and boasted as to how he was going to quieten the noisy dog. He bet that he could do it; some money changed hands as we all thought he would fail. Alec arrived back from lunch and asked us to take note of what he was going to do; he showed us a small block of chocolates called Laxettes. I had been given these when I was a kid to make me regular. Just half a little square from the block was enough to have me running to the loo two or three times in a row.

We all followed Alec through the boundary to the caravan. The dog had heard us and was really getting excited; he was in the barking, scratching, and snarling mode. Alec took the silver paper wrapping off the small block and inserted it under the door of the caravan. The dog stopped barking and came to the door to see what had been put under the door; we could hear him chewing it up. As soon as the dog finished the chocolate bar, he resumed his ceaseless barking. We were confident of winning some money from this deal.

We were all starting to pick up our tools and were quietly confident that we had won the bet when the WOOF WOOF WOOF ended in a Woo. The dog had stopped barking.

We realized that we had lost our money. It was almost worth it to be able to work in silence. I had changed my name for Alec to Smart Alec, a derogatory Australian slang term for smart-arse.

The young German couple rode onto the block. Still, the dog was silent. The young man opened the caravan door and yelled to his partner, "Scheiser, Der Hund mit Scheiser. " He dragged the poor dog out of the caravan; he was covered in it. We could smell him from where we were working.

The dog was tied to a chain, and a lot of the gear in the van was carried outside. This was squirted down with a garden hose, as was the dog.   The young man came across to us and asked if we would have some offcut timber to build a dog house. He did not want the big dog to be in the caravan during the day.

I think Smart Alec must have felt a bit guilty as he and his men helped the guy to build a large dog kennel.

After this episode, the dog, which was on a running lead, spent a lot of his time in the kennel and did not bark at all. We used to go over to him, give him some of our lunch, and pat him.

The dead humpback whale

The fishing trip with friends had us past Reeveseby Island out from Tumby Bay in South Australia. We were on a quest to catch King George Whiting to replenish our empty freezer. There were three couples on the twenty-five-foot Bertram boat.

The fishing in the area known locally as the Lagoon had been a disappointment as we had only caught one small leatherjacket. We decided to travel around the outside of the island to the easterly shore to try there.

As the day progressed, the fishing had improved somewhat; we had two dozen nice large fish in the Esky on ice. Mary was looking out to sea. I asked her what she was looking at. 'I think there is a large upturned boat floating about a mile out to the east'; I looked where she was pointing and could also see the curved outline of what looked like the bottom of a boat.

We pulled the anchor and set off toward the boat; as we neared the object floating, we realized that this was a dead whale or some other large sea creature. As we came closer, we realized that the creature was indeed a dead whale.

We decided to drive around the carcass to see if we could identify the species. This was a big mistake. As we got downwind of the whale, the smell nearly took our breath away. We had ascertained by now that this was a Humpback whale from the size of its fins and the shape of the body.

I drove the boat right up to the side of the whale when we were upwind to get a good look at the large dead creature. We were marveling at the size of the whale, and as we were both drifting, we were almost touching the carcass all of the time.

Suddenly a huge grey shape shot out of the water right next to our boat. It hit the side of the boat as it passed us, almost knocking us over. This was a huge White Pointer shark. As the shark slid down the side of the whale, it chewed huge hunks of blubber from the carcass.

We reversed the boat away thirty meters and watched the spectacle of the eighteen-foot shark gorging itself with the blubber. The shark was then joined by a slightly smaller one that was also eating the carcass. I had a camera with me and took a lot of photos of the feeding sharks. This was a scene I had never seen before in all of my years of fishing in this area.

We left the scene of the feeding sharks and returned to our fishing east of Reeveseby Island and caught another three dozen whiting.   It is surprising what one sees in the ocean. The vast areas must really have some tales to tell.

In The Poo Again

It was in about December nineteen sixty- two. Three days before Christmas, many tradespeople had an end-of-year drink together at one of the local Port Lincoln hotels. The usual choice was the old Port Lincoln Hotel.

My stepdaughter Mary had just married one of my apprentices, Bob. After finishing a plumbing job in the morning, we headed off to see all of our mates at the pub. Bob and I loaded the tools into the old Commer work ute and drove off to the pub.

The publican had put on a lot of finger food and had some hot pies and pasties for all of the patrons to thank them for their patronage during the year. I usually did most of the plumbing works at the local hotels. The son-in-law was a top football player in the town, as he always told everyone he met. His voice could be heard spruiking his prowess with the ball and other things as the afternoon progressed. Quite a few free beers had been downed by this time as the publican had donated an eighteen-gallon Keg for the occasion.

As the night progressed, the publican asked me about fixing the hotel septic tank system, which evidently had some sort of blockage. I offered to have a look at this job before I went home. The publican said it could wait, even though the tank was overflowing onto the ground, causing a nasty smell. I insisted that I would look now.

As I left to look at the tank, Bob and a couple of mates followed the manager and me outside to check the problem.

The septic tank in the hotel was a very large one to take all of the mess from the guests and the kitchen. I could see that there was some seepage from one of the breather pipes. I went to the lid of the tank and, with a heave, lifted the concrete lid from the tank. Under normal circumstances, I would not have done this as the tank was over full.

The mixture of garden and food scraps, plus the unmentionables which the tank is used to clean, flowed out around my feet. I went to step back/ My foot slipped in the slimy mess. I slithered into the tank feet first, and I was not too pleased when my head went under the goo. I clawed my way to the top and took a deep breath; at least I had kept my mouth tightly closed during my ungainly dive. I took a breath and grabbed the edge of the tank but could not get a grip due to the slimy mess. Bob, who had been laughing his head off, as were his mates, carefully reached down and grabbed my shirt collar, and with one heave, hauled me out.

As I hit the ground, he and his mates quickly stepped back to make sure that they were not splattered with the unmentionable muck. 'I've lost my bloody glasses. ' I am sure not looking for them,' said Bob as he and his mates headed back to the bar.

I scraped as much of the s...t of with my hands and staggered to the Commer ute. I had trouble getting the keys out of the pocket of my overalls. The pockets seemed to be full of something else. With a sloppy scrunching noise, I sat in the ute seat. I opened the two windows to try to let some fresh air in and then drove off home.

The ute was parked in the front of our house; I climbed the steps onto the front veranda. Then rang the bell as well as knocked on the door. My wife Jean came to the door. When she opened it, she reeled back in horror. " don't you come inside, "she said in a menacing tone. "Get out on the lawn," I meekly obeyed. "Take all of your clothes off." I meekly did this, except for my underpants. She then got the hose and squirted

me down for about ten minutes. She had the pressure spraying nozzle going flat out.

I went into the rear shower cubicle and had a long hot shower, with plenty of soapsuds from a nice smelling bar of soap. The smell was up to my nose; I could still smell myself.

Jean came out to the back with a plate of food. "You can eat your tea with the dogs. Don't expect to sleep in the bed with me for a few days". I think she was pretty grumpy at the time. I ate the meal then went to bed on the small bed in the back room.

I had a good reminder of the escapade the next morning when I opened the ute door. The smell had gotten even worse during the night, even though the windows were left down all night. I would have no problems with anyone stealing the ute that night.

I have since read that a famous poet Tom Black had some swimming lessons in this same septic many years ago. Tom had a propensity to be known to consume large tomes of alcohol on occasions. On most occasions, when another was paying the bill.

Navigation problems

The engineering business in Adelaide was a good money earner, but the stress of running it was not doing my health any favors. I really needed a cat to kick or some other form of release from the daily grind.

A mate phoned one day and said that he had just the cure. A small island was for sale. It was only two kilometers off the coast in South Australia. This sounded interesting to me as, If I had a small power- boat, I could go and hide from the stress of work for a few days.

I phoned the land agent and arranged a viewing of the island. The island also had its own boat on a mooring on the mainland. We went to have a look at the island. There was a house of sorts, a small shearing shed, a tractor, and an old motor bike, plus a very early model T Ford car, which had just about rusted away.

After lunch at one of the town's hotels with the agent and a few steadying ales, I bought the little island. We went back to his office to sign the papers and pay the asking price.

The owner of the island, whose family had owned it for many years, offered to look after the island for me when I was away. He would also maintain the boat. This sounded like a very good deal. Clem was a bachelor and did not drink alcohol. He lived close to where the boat was moored.

My mate Kevin and I went out to the island on the boat to christen it. We had the mandatory cases of beer and some flagons of port wine.

The christening took a few days as we were not really capable of rowing out to the boat until the supplies had run out. There was one big problem. There was no way to keep the beer cold.

When I returned to shore, I asked Clem about the problem. Clem had just the thing stored in his shed. A kerosene refrigerator,

These refrigerators were powered by a tank of kerosene with a lamp wick; the heat from the lamp would cause the ammonia in the refrigerator to freeze the pipes in the small freezing compartment in the main cooler box.

My mate Kevin came to help with the situation with his small trailer. One problem with kerosene refrigerators was that they were extremely heavy, like a large Pianola.

We gut-busted the frig into the trailer and headed for the mooring. With a huge amount of effort, we loaded the refrigerator into the small tender dinghy. There was only about three inches' free board. I looked at the dinghy; it would not take my weight to row out to the boat. I waded out to the boat and drove back to where Kevin had the painter rope for towing.

We were heading for the island. A bit of wind had come up. The sea water became quite rough. Kevin looked back. "Hey, the dinghy has broken free." I slowed the motor down and went to the stern to look? "The rope is still tied on." I pulled the rope; it had a lot of tension on it. I looked back and could see the dinghy in the shallow water behind us being towed along by the boat.

We towed the submerged dinghy to the island and got as close to the shore as we could. Kevin got off the boat. I went to the mooring and tied up the boat. I swam ashore, walked to the homestead, cranked the old kerosene tractor to life, hooked the trailer on, then drove down onto the beach, then reversed back to Kevin and the dinghy. The dinghy was towed by hooking a rope to the trailer.

The fridge was really heavy now as a lot of the glass wool insulation had got wet. We finally had the fridge on the trailer after almost breaking our backs lifting it.

Back at the homestead, we tossed a few buckets of fresh water from the rainwater tank outside the house into and over the fridge. It was slid off the trailer near the door to the house. When the water had stopped dripping out of the sides of the fridge, it was carried inside and placed in the corner of the kitchen. We both had extremely sore backs.

We had a four-gallon tin of lighting kerosene just for the lamps with the mantles, which we used at night. Kevin filled the kerosene tank; I adjusted the wick out to wipe the water off it. After waiting for a short while, I lit the lamp. The tank was slid on its roller back under the flue. A short time later, I opened the door and felt the freezer; it had ice on it.

We had solved one problem. The fridge was stocked with bottles of hot beer which had been left from the last trip. We had to stop drinking this beer as the hot bottles shot most of the contents out when opened. This was wasting beer.

We looked down to the beach to see that the tide had gone out, and the dinghy was high and dry on the sand. We took some buckets and bailed it out, ready for the higher tide. The painter's rope was tied to a heavy rock to act as an anchor.

The beer supply ran out early in the night; there was a moon shining over the water. Kevin suggested that we travel back to the mainland and get some more supplies.

We paddled the now floating dinghy out to the boat; it was tied to the stern; I started the motor Kevin cast off the mooring rope and buoy. Kevin was sitting in the cabin. The lights of the town were going around in circles. The small town's lights would pass, then the lights of the large town would pass, the compass had gone crazy, slowly going round and round.

Finally, the problem was found. When Kevin had cast off the rope with the buoy had snagged around the cathead on the bow, we were still hooked to the moorings.

A chauffeur's tale

In my early days, when jobs were very hard to come by, I was very lucky to obtain employment with a wealthy Adelaide family as a chauffeur. The family had huge land holdings all over South Australia. Some of the large holdings were around Port Augusta, and others were near Port Lincoln. A lot of the agricultural land was in an undeveloped state with large areas of Mallee scrub and gum trees growing on it. Areas around Coffin Bay were used for grazing.

There was a homestead and sheds at Coffin Bay which was only accessed by a very rough narrow lane through the Mallee scrub. The family-owned a Rolls Royce car in Adelaide. The main part of my job was to drive Mrs. Mort lock around town on her errands. I felt very proud sitting in the chauffeur's seat in the open, in front of the sedan body where the Mort lock family rode.

Most of my driving entailed taking Mrs. Mortlock to charity events and shopping for clothes. Before I parked the car in the garage for the night, I would check to see if there was and dust or mud stuck to the body and wheels.

There was one bane to my job which I really hated. This was caused by the many stray dogs in the city area of Adelaide. It did not matter where I was in the city. The Rolls Royce acted as a magnet for them to come and urinate on the shiny chrome spokes in the wheels. Every night I had to carefully clean the dust which stuck to the smelly dog urine. While waiting for Mrs. Mortlock, one day, I was speaking about my problem to another chauffeur, who was leaning on the mudguard of his boss' car, cleaning a few spots off the windshield. My conversation turned to the dirty habits of the stray dogs

This guy had really taken the dog problem to another level. He had installed a box with trembler coils in it which came from an early model T model Ford. This box supplied the high power for the electric spark to fire the engine. He had told me how to set this up and assured me that this would be the end of my problem. Evidently, these cunning strays had a few brains when they selected cars to pee on. The guy had no problems after a few of the dogs had been given a powerful shock through the stream of urine they were squirting on the wheels. They had left in a hurry, howling like banshees.

I managed to find a coil off a crashed Model T Ford and attached it to the car battery via a switch. The other end of the coil had a weight and some wire which I lowered onto the roadway to act as an earth for the machine. I was ready for the first victim.

I was parked outside of John Martins in Rundle Street in Adelaide. This seemed to be the dog's favorite haunt. I had opened the rear door and held Mrs. Mortlock's hand to guide her to the ground. When I returned to my seat, I was intently watching through the mirror and to the side of the car for my first victim.

A very large ugly, dirty dog approached the car. I had seen the victim on many occasions; this dog seemed to have an endless supply of pee. Just before this dog lifted his leg, I turned the switch on; I saw the long stream of yellow urine squirt toward the tire and wheel. The hair on the dirty dog's body all rose up; he swung around and bit at his penis, letting out a huge roar as he did so. The dog then took off, howling as he did so, he ran straight through the door of John Martins Store.   Mrs. Mortlock was just leaving the store. The large dog ran straight between her legs and knocked her to the ground. Parcells was strewn askew. I was transfixed with horror. Mrs. Mortlock got to her feet, one of the John Martin employees picked up her shopping. It was like something unfolding in slow motion. I should have been waiting to stow the shopping, then open the door and help her into the car.

Mrs. Mortlock grabbed at the door handle of the car. Her hair shot out from her head. I quickly turned the coil off and ran to her assistance. As she sat herself down in the car, I quickly tried to explain to her about the dog problem. She was not interested. She had been made a laughing stock in the main street of Adelaide.

I was thankful that Mrs. Mortlock could not drive as I think she would have gotten into my seat and left me standing in the street. "Young man, you will not be working for us anymore." She said with venom in her voice.

That afternoon I was summoned to the boss, Mr. William Mortlock's office. I was sure I was going to lose my job. I was made to stand in front of his large desk and explain what had happened. I told him in a quivery voice about the dog problem. As I spoke, I noticed a sign of a smile. He opened a cigar case the selected a large cigar then lit it. He had a smile on his face.

"Now, young man, that would have been a sight I would have liked to witness. Do not ever repeat this, or you will definitely lose your job. Just be careful in the future when you try to fry any more dogs".

Percy's swim with the sharks

It was a beautiful February day, a light breeze was blowing, and the sun was shining, A perfect fishing day in the sheltered waters of Boston Bay, Port Lincoln, South Australia.

My brother Fred and I had been pestering Father all week about using the twenty-three-foot fishing cutter for a fishing trip around the bay. We had heard that a few mates had caught some snapper near Spalding Cove.

The boat was moored in Proper Bay. A small dinghy was on a running line at Snook's Landing, about a mile from our house. The dinghy was used to ferry the goods and passengers out to the boat, which was moored about forty meters off shore.

There were four of us, and we were really looking forward to this trip out sailing in the boat; the two mates were Percy and Bob. They had been invited to school during the week.

As we walked around to Snook's landing, we talked about some fishing stories and wondered if the fish were still biting, as they evidently had been during the week; we were really looking forward to the day sailing in the bay.

We paddled the dinghy out to the cutter, stowed our fishing gear and lunch on board, then tied the short painter rope on the dinghy to the mooring rope with the buoy tied to it. Percy cast the mooring off, and Fred pulled the jib up to get underway while we undid all of the ties holding the cover on the main sail. The cutter started to sail beautifully.

We tacked over toward Boston Island, as the light breeze was coming from the Brothers Islands, which were near to where the fish was meant to be coming from. After we had almost arrived at Fanny Point on Boston Island, went on another tack toward the Brothers, there was a shallow area near them called the Sunken Brother.

Fred and I lined up the fishing marks, the point of one island over some rocks at the distant shore, and another being a tree over the start of a sandy beach. As we arrived at our destination, I pointed the cutter into the wind and dropped the main sail. Percy tossed the anchor into the water. We left the jib set as this was not in the way, and it was going to save some effort when we were going to leave.

We got our fishing lines out of the bag, baited the hooks, then lowered them into the water; almost straight away, Bob caught a nice Snapper about three pounds in weight, we all started to catch fish and had quite a few in the well of the boat.

Fred was pulling up a large snapper when his line went loose; He pulled the line in to find the head of the fish left on the hook. We all did the same. We baited up again; the same thing happened; we could see the shape of the shark in the water as it chased the fish before biting it off the hook. The

Shark looked fairly large, possibly a White Pointer, from the blotchy markings we could see in the gloom.

We had a unanimous decision to leave, as we did not want this shark to get too friendly. Percy started to pull the heavy anchor up as we set about getting the mainsail ready to hoist. Just as Percy had the anchor on board, a strong puff of wind gibed the jib. We could not see Percy behind the sail; we were busy pulling the mainsail up.

The next thing we noticed was Percy grabbing the stern of the boat and climbing aboard. The jib had knocked him overboard with the shark. We mentioned this to Percy, whose answer was." I did not even get wet."   We sailed off and left the shark to find his own food. Then went across to the Homestead near Point Donnington, where we caught some nice King George Whiting.

Old Stinky the kangaroo

We had quite a few free loaders on our farm; there were Parrots and crows in the fruit garden. Crows and foxes around the sheep, mainly during the lambing season, Galahs and Kangaroos and crows in the harvest season. All seemed to want to eat, maim, or kill our farm animals, or roll in our crops

The crow was an extremely cunning creature. It would sit on a hill or a tree and watch as the sheep grazed, looking for something they could feast on. I was checking the ewes one day and, from a distance, saw a crow fly up to a ewe just dropping a newborn lamb. The crow instantly hopped onto the lamb before the ewe could get up and pecked through the newborn lamb's skin and pulled something out, and flew off. No wonder we were losing lambs.

The next morning, I took some old rendered fat from the refrigerator out, plus a syringe full of liquid sheep dip when I checked on the ewes and lambs. I put a dab of the rendered fat on top of a tall post and squirted some of the sheep dip into the middle of it. As we drove around the paddock checking the sheep, I noticed one dead lamb. It was early in the morning, and the crows had not pecked the eyes out yet, so I inserted the syringe and injected a dose of the sheep dip into the eye socket. As we were driving away, my wife noticed a crow hopping up to the dead lamb; we stopped to watch; he dove his beak into the eye, then pulled it out and started to walk around wiping his beak in the green pasture, another crow landed and did the same.

We went to check the sheep the next morning to find fifteen patches of black feathers in the paddock where the foxes had cleaned the dead crows up from the night before. I would like to think that these cruel killers would have been wiping their noses on the ground and walking backward as well. The dead lamb was removed the next morning so the farm dogs would not get poisoned.

The fox would kill small newborn lambs and also attack a sheep if the sheep were not able to get to its feet for some reason. The fox would eat the udder out of the living sheep then eat out its tongue. Foxes would also burrow under the netting of the chicken run and, just for fun, kill most of the chickens. If it killed one of the chicken and ate it, one would not mind so much

 The evil crows would also peck the eyes out of a live sheep as it was lying on the ground, unable to get to its feet. They also liked fruit from the fruit trees in the garden. Another one of their treats was to steal the eggs from the fowl run. If a crow was to sit in a tree near a shed where one had a gun, it always seemed to know if you were loading the gun. Before you could sight the gun on the crow, it flew off.

 One had to be as cunning as a crow to shoot one, this bird has a sixth sense, but as most cunning creatures, they had a foible, which was usually fueled by greed.

We were harvesting a small paddock of oats, and the itchy screenings which had been screened off by the harvester were dropped onto the ground in a heap. I had finished reaping this paddock of oats and was going out to the harvester to check if the moisture of the grain was low enough so we could reap. The small pile of oats had about fifty crows sitting on it and spreading the heap out.

The moisture of the grain was far too high to reap, so we loaded up some steel fence pickets and some old rusty wire netting on the Ute. We drove out to the oat pile and scared the crows off; they sat in some small trees and on a stone heap and protested very loudly. I rolled the netting out in a circle of about three meters across and joined the ends, pricking my fingers as one usually does when doing this job, then the fence picket was knocked in to form the circle. Two pickets were placed in the middle of the circle to hold the netting roof on our coop. When it was finished, we cut a hole in the middle of the roof the size of a small hat brim. The idea was for the crows to jump in and not be able to fly out.

I had seen this idea in an old farmer's almanac many years ago. We had tried it in the chicken run with an egg on the ground for bait, and it had worked. I did not mind swapping one egg for a crow. The advantage was that if the crow were in the trap, his mates would see it and not come around, especially if the crow was hit on the head and killed then hung on the chicken run fence.

 We left the crow trap and went home. I waited for the temperature of the day to warm and kept my eye on the air moisture meter in the kitchen of the house. When I went out to start harvesting, I noticed about six crows in the trap gorging themselves on the oats.

The next morning, I went out early to check the trap; there were twenty crows in the trap. I had a piece of fencing wire with a bend on the end of it so I could hook the crows by the leg and pull them out under the netting to give them a tap on the head with a piece of a broom handle. This was ok, but the crows were getting a bit worried by this time and were climbing up the walls of the trap. I eventually made a small net on a handle and finally emptied the trap. The dead crows were bagged up and then tossed down an old mineshaft on the way home.

Every day we had between fifteen and twenty-five crows in this trap, which was dispatched to the old mine shaft until after about a week there was a hot morning, and I started to reap very early and did not empty the trap of crows. When I finished for the day, it was dark, and I was pretty tired .so the crows had an extra day of feeding in the trap.

We went out to empty the trap the next morning and noticed that the mob of crows that usually sat around the trap were nowhere to be seen.

The crows in the trap had changed voice from their greedy short caws that they made when feeding to a strident caw which was evidently an alarm sound. The day's crows were dispatched to the mine with their mates; these birds were the last crows that went into this trap for two weeks. The crows had vanished.

We had a small mob of kangaroos who were residents on the farm. They did a small amount of damage to the crops. It was usually the big mobs that alternated in numbers through the night that did the real damage. As I drove around to work and checked on the live- stock, I quite often saw a large buck kangaroo and about three does and a couple of joeys. He was one of the residents.

I was shifting a mob of sheep which had just been shorn along a track through a crop of wheat. As the sheep had been around the shearing shed for a couple of days, they were pretty hungry and were straying off from the track and knocking some crop down. Fred, the excellent sheep dog, would jump up and look where the sheep were, then run unseen through the crop, then jump up in front of the sheep to bring them back to the rest of the mob. We finally got the sheep through the crop into the new paddock. I followed them along for a bit to check on them. They were heading for the dam to get a drink. Fred ran ahead to get a drink and have a swim. I turned for home then shut the gate of the paddock. I really did not want Fred sitting on the petrol tank of the motorbike as most people know what a wet dog smells like, especially a farm dog, who usually has some lovely things to roll in, like a cowpat or some sort of dead animal. I was being a bit cunning as I did not mind him having a ride if he had run for a while and dried off a bit.

I was heading home and smelled the really rank smell of the old kangaroo. He smelled very much like a Billy-goat. Old stinky was lazily hopping along the fence line with his kids and harem. He was at the back of the mob. I was being a bit smart, so I decided to rev the bike up and get behind Stinky. I was about three meters behind him revving the motor; Stinky was not phased a bit, he just kept hopping along at his pace, when suddenly he half turned to look at me, then took a giant leap and landed next to me, then put his arms with the big long claws around my chest and grabbed me. I nearly fell off the bike; I had got a real scare, for I had heard of people being grabbed by a kangaroo before. If one was on the ground, they rip with their hind legs, but they also claw with the front legs and bite with their large teeth. I would have made some of the bike racing experts proud; I gunned the motor and was nearly laying on my side when old Stinky's claws were dragged off me. I roared off for a short distance, then stopped and turned around. Old Stinky had stopped hopping and was looking my way. His shoulders were humping up and down. I am sure he was laughing at me. Fred caught up to me at this time and was dry enough to carry home on the bike.

Shark Feeding Frenzy

Finally, the wind had slowed down. The Elliston area of South Australia was well known for the long periods of southwesterly to southeasterly winds. Good windmill country the area was described as. The place did have a very large number of windmills in the district as the limestone soil and the large stony areas had very good water under them at, in most cases, a shallow depth.

A mate and I had been hanging out for a day's fishing to supplement the dwindling supplies of fish in the freezer. The windy weather had been blowing for at least ten days. The sea was very rough, with a large swell coming into the bay.

We launched our fifteen-foot boat at Anxious Bay and headed towards Waldegrave Island. There was some large whiting to be caught in the cold waters around this island.

On the point of Waldegrave was a huge red granite rock that looked very much like a huge Sperm Whale; we called this Whale Rock. The rock had a seal colony living on and around it. The seals were interesting to watch as they played by sliding down the side of the rock into the sea. They would climb back on the slippery rock to repeat the fun of the water slide.

We started to fish about fifty meters out from the rock and were catching some nice Whiting and a few Tommy Roughs. Occasionally a seal would swim out to the boat and swim around it to check us out. Sometimes the seal would put on a show for us by diving down then leaping out of the water next to us. The tricks the seals did on occasions were similar to the trained seals in the cities, which wowed the paying patrons with their antics. We got this for free.

We had one very clever seal about ten meters from our boat going through a very good routine. We were enthralled by how clever this wild creature was. He was lying on top of the water watching us pull in a nice fish when a huge dark shape lurched out of the water with its mouth open and grabbed him. The shark then tossed him into the air, then dove down and picked the mortally wounded seal up, and repeated the same maneuver. This went on a few times. We were quickly pulling the anchor up and starting the outboard motor.

We went about two miles away and started to fish again. This shark was at least the same size as our boat, if not a few feet longer. We did not want to meet up with him again.

Pussy Cat Tales

Father had acquired a fox terrier dog. It was a female we called Trixie. My brother, sisters, and I had a lot of fun with this energetic little dog. We would take her chasing rabbits in the scrubby land that surrounded our house; she occasionally caught one.

Trixie really liked chasing the neighbor's cats as well, although she was not too keen on catching one of these. I had been out with Trixie one day when she did catch Mrs. Murphy's tomcat; Trixie had come off second best in this fight. Like most kids, I had egged her on to chase this cat. Trixie lost a bit of skin from the scratches, plus had a few nasty bite marks on her. I got some bites and scratches when I tried to stop the fight.

We had another cat called Tommy. I did not like him very much, as, like a lot of cats, especially tom cats, he was prone to scratch and bite. One minute he would be lying on my knee purring; the next minute, he would scratch and bite.

When, as all-female creatures usually do, the dog came on heat, father took her to one of the neighbors to mate her with the people's fox terrier dog.

I wanted to accompany my father; he had become quite gruff when I had asked if I could go with him.

The time the puppies should arrive had been talked about after father had brought the dog home. Every day I studied the dog to see if she was getting any bigger.

At last, the dog started to get a droopy udder along her belly and was noticeably bigger. Finally, the day arrived. I came home from school to be told that Trixie had six beautiful puppies; she was in a basket in the laundry.

I was a bit taken aback at first when one went in to see Trixie; she had bared her teeth and had snapped at me. Mother later informed me that this was the usual thing for a new mother to do as she did not know if I was going to hurt her puppies.

The puppies grew quickly and were soon playing around the yard. They made a mess digging holes in father's garden. This did not amuse him very much. He usually growled and said nasty things about the pups.

I knew that father was not really that angry with the pups as I noticed that he quite often picked one or two up and played with them. The puppies were about six weeks old, and on this particular Sunday afternoon, after dinner, Father asked one of the lodgers if he would help to dock the tails of the puppies.

Father got a block of hardwood and a butcher's knife; he also had a thick piece of round kindling which was used to start the wood fire each morning.

The puppies were grabbed one by one, and then their tails were held over the piece of hardwood. The knife was then put on the joint off the tail where the docking was to take place. The knife was then hit with a piece of kindling wood. The tail quivered on the ground for a while after it had been severed, not unlike a rooster's head after it had been cut off. The puppies were all done; they were all back with Trixie, who was busily trying to lick their tails to make them better.

The black and white tomcat sauntered over and sat next to me. He had his usual cat superior look on his face. I noticed that where he was sitting, his tail was resting on the piece of hardwood; the butcher's knife and piece of kindling were still next to it.

I barely had to move to reach the knife and wood. I held the knife over Tom's tail and gave it an almighty whack with the wood. Tom was not as docile as the small puppies had been. Tom let out a bloodcurdling shriek and took off. The recently severed tail thrashed around on the ground. Tom cleared the back fence in a giant leap and was gone. Father came out to pick the knife and wood up and was going to dispose of the puppy tails. He looked at the still wriggling black cat tail on the ground, then seriously at me. Here goes l thought another trip the bathroom and the razor strop. Father's shoulders started to shake with laughter; He squatted down because he was laughing so much. Phew, I thought, safe at last. I had gotten away with that trick.

The old tomcat did not come back. I think that his superior attitude had been compromised by not having his tail wag around when he was angry.

Shark For Dinner

The weather had been really rough for the last week. The strong wind had been blowing from the southeast at speeds of between twenty and thirty-five knots. This wind made finding shelter at the Neptune Islands hard to find. The large swell would sneak around the headland we were sheltering behind and make sleeping really difficult.

We left the shelter of the small cove and headed out with our forty-foot Rock lobster boat out into the wind and sea. I thought that the conditions had abated a little, but as we left the shelter, the waves proved me wrong. We headed south to where our lobster pots were set. We had to punch through the three-meter waves. As we did so, the nose of the boat dipped and tossed water back over the wheelhouse, giving the impression we were under the ocean. This was pretty scary stuff, even for an experienced fisherman like my mate and me.

If we were to leave the pots to seek shelter at a better place, the long trip there and back was very costly in fuel and time. If the pots were left too long, we found we had unwanted visitors like seals or large octopus or fish, which were all fond of the taste of the expensive Rock Lobster meat. We arrived at the grounds where we had set the pots and found the long pole with the flag, which denoted the starting point to pick up the pots. The bin of cut-up Australian Salmon for bait was secured, ready to

change the bait in the traps before they were dropped back into the ocean.

The line was pulled aboard with the small grapnel and rope, which hooked the line behind the first of two buoys. The rope was put onto the rotating winch wheel, which towed the pot out to the boat. When the pot came alongside, it was dragged onto a tipping cradle which lifted the pot and held it on a table-like section of the cradle. The lobsters were removed, and then the old and new bait were changed over.   The first pot had four large lobsters, which were at that time worth about one hundred dollars each. When a new suitable pinnacle of rock showed on the paper of our echo sounder, the now re-baited pot was dropped back into the ocean.

The second pot hauled aboard had three empty lobster shells and one lobster without any legs in it; the pot also held a very large octopus that had eaten three of the lobsters and frightened the other, making it drop its legs. I had a special hate for the then worthless octopus. This one had just cost me over three hundred dollars; I grabbed the large octopus around the body just above the tentacles; I pulled him quickly from the pot and tossed him at the large hot exhaust, which led to the Gardiner diesel engine which drove the boat. The octopus's tentacles wound around the hot exhaust and cooked him to the pipe. This was almost instant death.

We worked our way along the line of pots in the heaving ocean swell picking up our pots and resetting them back into the ocean. We had to be extremely careful not to get one of the ropes snagged on the propeller.

To do this in the huge sea might have ended up a disaster.

The cartons of bait in the cold room were getting very short. There were only two left. The wet well on the boat had plenty more room for lobsters

When we sheltered for the night, I had an idea about how to supplement our dwindling bait room. I took a heavy rope with a length of heavy chain and a large shark hook on its end; I tied the rope to the sternpost of the boat and then baited the hook with some of the cooked octopus from the now cooled exhaust pipe. I dropped this over the side of the boat before we went to our bunks for the night. I had used this idea before and had caught a few bronze whaler sharks and had used their flesh for bait.

My mate and I were tucked up in our bunks with the lee sheet tied up to stop us from rolling out of bed. I was having a nice dream of being home out of the joggling sea. All hell broke loose the boat was being shaken like a rabbit with a large dog clamped onto it.

My mate was getting out of bed as well; we dressed and put on some heavy waterproof clothes, then I turned on the large floodlight which lit up the rear deck of the boat.

There was an amazing scene in front of us, and a huge white pointer shark was hooked; it was shaking the boat violently as it tried to get away. I turned and went to get the .303 rifle which was wrapped up in oiled rags. This was kept especially for this type of problem. I returned with the gun and fired three shots into the top of the shark's head; This quietened him down considerably. We went back to sleep.

At first light, I sent a message on the radio offering free bait. I had four responses to the call. I thought that there were only three boats working in this region. I tied a heavy rope to the line with the shark hooked and put the end around the anchor winch, then winched the large shark to the bow of the boat. We then put a rope around him with great effort and lifted the huge creature alongside and half out of the water. Just as we finished, the first boat arrived, the guys started to help butcher the shark. Finally, with the ten men working, we had reduced the shark to mainly a skeleton. Large slabs of meat were being transferred from boat to boat to fill the iceboxes with bait.

The final job was to remove the huge jaws from this large shark. These jaws from sharks of this size were worth a lot of money. I wanted to tan them to keep in my lounge room high up on the wall. The jaws were stowed in the ice.

I have had some interesting comments about these huge shark jaws when visitors enter my home.

Auntie Alice RIP

I was excited. The school holidays were approaching, and mother had promised that I could go and stay on my uncle and aunt's farm at Maitland in South Australia.

For a ten-year-old, this was going to be a real adventure, my first long-term staying away from home. I really liked Uncle Fred and Aunt Margaret. They had two girls. I was a bit worried about this.

The day soon arrived. I was taken to the bus depot and put on the bus bound for the Yorke Peninsula. The bus driver had instructions to let me off at Maitland and to make sure I picked up my small suitcase full of clothes.

I had been to uncle and aunties' farm on many occasions and had even tentatively made friends with the two girls, Maud was a year older than me, and Ruby was a year younger. These two girls seemed a bit different than the prissy girls who went to our school in Adelaide

The bus finally pulled into the depot at Maitland. I was covered with dust from the dry dirt roads we had been traveling on since leaving Adelaide; Aunt Margaret was waiting, and she collected my suitcase and walked with me to the car. This car was a large, almost new Buick Straight Eight. Father was always talking about rich Uncle Fred and all of the farms he owned.

The farmhouse was, in my eyes, a real mansion. It had rows of rose bushes and a neatly cut lawn in the front. As we arrived, I noticed one of the workmen tending the garden.

The two girls came out of the house to greet me. Both had been riding their ponies and were quite dirty, very different than the prissy Adelaide girls, I thought.

Auntie ushered me into a large bedroom near the kitchen and unpacked my case for me. This room had a large shiny brass double bed and well-maintained antique furniture; there was a beautiful marble washstand and a pretty bowl and jug on the top, wicker chairs, and large polished wardrobes with mirrors in the doors.

I spent the afternoon trying to learn to ride one of the ponies and had fallen off a few times, and only my pride had been hurt by this. The girls were really helpful and friendly, a bit unusual for girls, I thought.

Uncle had been supervising the reaping of the crops on the farms and had arrived home in the early dusk. After dinner, I was really tired and went off to bed. I did have a few bruises from my falls off the horse, but I was not going to admit that was I was sore from my poor riding skills.   Being very tired, I had drifted off to sleep almost as soon as my head had hit the pillow; I was having a marvelous dream about galloping the horses around the farm.

I woke up with a start as the room had suddenly turned freezing cold. This was summertime, and it seemed strange to me. There was a dim light in the room, which prior to this had been pitch dark. I turned over and saw a pretty woman in a lace nightgown at the end of my bed. She was watching me with hollow eyes very intently. She moved around the room to the side of the bed. She did not move her legs; she just floated in the air. She then moved to the wardrobe to check herself in the mirror on the door. I could see that there was no reflection in the mirror. I was transfixed by this specter and was afraid to move. The aura of the pretty lady started to dim, and the room was again pitch black and quickly warming up again. I thought I should be brave and not scream out as I really wanted to do.

Auntie knocked on the door of my room to tell me that breakfast was ready. I could hear the roosters crowing in the chicken coop behind the house yard.

I dressed and washed my hands and face in the bathroom, then went to the kitchen for the bacon and eggs I could smell. As I sat at the table, auntie noticed that I had a funny look on my face. "Oh, I am sorry, Rex, did you see Auntie Alice last night". Auntie explained that Auntie Alice had been uncle Fred's auntie and had died in that room after she had fallen off a horse on the farm many years ago.   Auntie moved me to another room and shut the door on Auntie Alice's room.

I surely did not open it for the next two weeks while I was staying on the farm. I even walked along the other side of the passage when I passed it.

Short-sighted shark

The tuna fishing was slow. We had used a lot of our pilchards to chum the tuna for a very small result. As we were getting low on bait, we decided to camp at the Neptune Islands for the night and hang a large bright light over the stern of the tuna boat to try to attract some small fish to net and augment our chum bait.

The weather was calm, and it was a very nice evening. Two of us were watching and occasionally dipping the large dab net to catch some of the fish. Another boat was doing the same as us, trying to catch some fish. One of the guys on the other boat must have been looking to have a crap; he Climbed down onto the tuna catching platform on the stern. He then pulled his pants down and hung his behind over the water. We were watching him when suddenly a huge great white shark shot out of the water, sliding past the bare backside, it hit the transom of the boat with a thud making the boat rock wildly.

The large shark slid down the edge of the tuna platform, then slowly sank back into the water. The fisherman had leaped back on the boat deck in one bound. The guy was then running around yelling and screaming profanities and rubbing his bare bottom, tripping on his trousers as he ran.

The skin on a shark is very similar to sandpaper. The guy had his rear end badly grazed by the sharkskin, plus the speed in which it had been applied would have burnt him with the friction. Suddenly the fifty-foot tuna boat was being tossed around in the water.

Evidently, the shark must have been angry at missing out on such an easy meal; it had hold of the rudder and was violently shaking the boat. When we arrived back in Port Lincoln, we told some mates about this experience and were scoffed at as being liars. The guy on the other boat had shown off his sandpapered rump. No one believed him or us. Two months later, when the boat was on the slipway being cleaned down for a new paint job, the jagged marks could be seen in the rudder of the boat. A huge shark tooth was embedded into the timber section of the rudder. It was carefully prized out with a thin knife.

I have seen a lot of shark teeth in all of my fishing years; this tooth was the biggest tooth I have ever seen.

This was told to me by Joe, a professional tuna fisherman who has fished for sixty years.

Bees In The Chimney

The women were washing the dishes after an enjoyable Sunday roast with John Henry and Jean, my in-laws, and Jim and Maureen, my wife's sister and husband.

John had just produced a bottle of Johnny Walker Whisky for a small swig to help the food digest.

The front passage doorbell rang. John walked up the passage and answered the door; he returned with a long-time next-door neighbor Auntie Elsie, who shared part of the house next door with her sister and husband. The trio were relations to Johns's sister Thelma.

Poor Elsie was in a state, her chimney had a swarm of bees in it, and they were coming down into her house. Jim, my brother-in-law, was an expert on almost everything, or so he used to say; he promised that the bees would be gone in no time.

Johnnie had a large shed behind his house, where he used to make rainwater tanks before he retired from plumbing; we all left the kitchen to the shed to work out the best method of attack. Auntie Elsie left for home to await the drastic action to remove the bees.

Jim had a really good idea as to getting rid of unwanted bees; this involved a pump-up garden sprayer filled with petrol. The sprayer was filled then the long wooden extension ladder was taken down from the hooks on the back of the shed.

Everything that Jim did was always done in a hurry; it did not pay to get in his way; Johnnie and I carried the ladder while he carried the sprayer.

As soon as we got to Elsie's house, Jim had the ladder propped up against the chimney. The bottom of the ladder was stood on the spongy Buffalo Grass lawn, which grew out from the wall of the house. The ladder was extended out as the top of the tall chimney was about six meters high.

Jim ran up the rungs of the ladder while holding the petrol-filled sprayer.

He started to pump and spray the bees. Unbeknown to us, Elsie had returned to her lounge room to keep an eye on the proceedings and to spray any errant bees which had entered the room with fly spray. Elsie had a brilliant, fail-safe method to get rid of the bees. She went to the kitchen and got some newspaper and rolled it into balls, then placed it into the fireplace. She lit the paper with a match.

Johnnie and I were holding the ladder steady as Jim was spraying. The next minute there was a loud boom, and flames shot out of the top of the chimney. Jim was lifted off the ladder and tumbled down, just missing Johnnie and me, and landed on his back on the lawn. We ran to see if he was all right. Just as we did so, the top two rows of bricks that had been dislodged from the top of the chimney started to land all around us. We were very lucky none of them had hit us as they had traveled a fair way higher than the chimney to before falling back to earth. Jim had had the wind knocked out of him but appeared to be ok; the very spongy lawn had broken his fall.

Our next concern was for Elsie; we both left Jim and rushed into the house to check on her condition. Elsie was sitting on the floor of her lounge room with her back hard up against the wall, her face was red, and her hair singed. She, too, had appeared to be all right, luckily. The women had rushed out of the house upon hearing the explosion and had come to see if Elsie were ok; they helped her to sit upon the lounge chair. Jean went to the bathroom and returned with some face cream to smear on her face. Johnnie and I adjourned to the lawn to check on Jim.

Jim was sitting up on the lawn; he had a red face and singed hair as well. We asked him if he was ok, he said he thought so. After about five minutes, he finally got to his feet. He was a bit unsteady for a while.   I left the men and went to see if Elsie was still ok. The three women and her sister were fussing over her; she seemed to be coming to her senses a bit more and had a bit of a laugh about the bees. I went to look up the chimney; there was not a bee to be seen.

The Carbide In The Bottle Trick

In the late nineteen-twenties, when I was a lad in Port Lincoln, swimming and fishing was all the go. We had not yet succumbed to the girl craze; they were only someone's big or little sister. The big sisters usually looked at us with disdain, while the little sisters were a damned pest.

One of my friends had overheard his big brother talking about a new way of catching fish. This new method involved some calcium carbide, a drink bottle with a marble in the neck as were in use at the time, and some sand.

The drink bottle had some calcium carbide tipped into the dry bottle, then some sand was added so the bottle would not float. The bottle was then dipped into the water and then quickly upended to seal the marble against the rubber ring in the neck. The bottle was then tossed amongst a school of fish.

Calcium carbide was readily available at this time, as it was used to create light on motorbikes and pushbikes (Bicycles). The lamp had a drip-feed for water to drip into the carbide in the lamp base. The water caused an acetylene gas to be produced. This was lit to provide light. We were living at the end of the jetty where father had a holding facility for his oyster business. I was the fish expert as I spent a lot of time on the Kirton Point Jetty, also a lot of time climbing under the jetty on the cross struts.

Large windjammer sailing ships would often be tied up at the jetties in town, picking up grain to take to Europe and other countries. There were gangs of wharfie's working in shifts to load these boats.

Tommy came to school one morning with a small can of calcium carbide, which he had borrowed without asking from his big brother. The weather was good, so we planned to go and get some fish the next day, which was Saturday.

We all congregated at the jetty. We had some bottles ready for the experiment. There were six of us. We each had a sugar bag to put the fish in.

A small amount of carbide was put into each of the bottles, and then the sand was added. We crawled under the jetty and walked around on the cross piles until we found a school of Tommy ruffs, a small tasty fish. I dipped my bottle in the water, then upended it and tossed it amongst the fish. The bottle sank down under the fish; BOOM. A plume of water shot up and hit the bottom of the jetty.

We scrambled around and picked the stunned fish up, and put them into a bag. Another school of fish was found. The bottle was dipped, then sealed, then tossed into the water. This bottle did not have enough sand in it and was still floating; we all tried to hide behind a jetty pile. The boom was twice as loud—pieces of broken glass ricochet among the jetty piles. One boy let out a piercing scream. He had been hit by a piece of glass. His ear was hanging by a small piece of skin. We climbed up a side ladder on the jetty, helping our wounded mate as we did.   The gang of Wharf workers loading the ship next to the other side of the wharf was not amused; they reached us as we climbed up to the top of the jetty and pulled us over the side. The big strong guy doing the pulling gave each one of us a huge hit under the ear, which nearly lifted our heads off, except for the wounded mate. One of the wharfies took his car up along the jetty and loaded him up for a trip to the hospital to have his ear stitched back.

As we walked away from the jetty, we decided that there were better ways to get fish. We had even left the bag with the fish in behind.

The small-town bush telegraph had worked very well. Father came home from work and grabbed me. " Ok, you, you're coming into the bathroom" I knew what lived in there. The blasted razor-strop.   At school the next day, we were not only the butt of a lot of jokes about us. I had a devil of a time sitting down for the next week.

The first Tipper Tray Truck

My brother-in-law jack had tendered for a contract to cart gravel for the start of building the new freezing works at Port Lincoln, South Australia. Times were pretty tough in the depression, so any work was really appreciated; Jack had a two-and-a-half-ton Bedford truck, which was lying idle more times than not.

The method of loading this truck was to have one person on each side of the truck shoveling the gravel onto the tray until the tray was full, and then a hungry board was fitted so we could load more material. Jack was left-handed, so we could watch each other and make a competition of tossing the gravel on board.

There was another contractor named Max who loaded his truck by himself. Max had a shovel almost twice the size of ours, and when we met up at the gravel pit, Max would keep up to the both of us loading his truck. When we had finished loading, we would cart our load to the building site and take the hungry boards off and shovel the load off onto the pile of gravel. Max would always keep up, Jack and I considered ourselves pretty fit, and it irked us that we could both be beaten by one man doing the job it took both of us to do. We would speed up when Max started to try and cut down the advantage, but Max would just raise his work rate as well. We could not beat him.

One morning Max rolled into work with a new truck. It had a frame behind the cabin with pulleys and steel cable; this led to a windlass-type winch with a ratchet dog to stop the tray from dropping down while the tray was being raised. Max would shovel a load of gravel onto the truck and drive to the site, back into the heap, and then wind the tray up with the winch apparatus. This took about a third of the time that it took us to shovel our load off. Max was making more money than both of us now as his unloading time was so much quicker. Jack and I were trying to work out how we could copy the new contraption so we could also earn more money.

The problem was that we would have to have taken the truck off the job to modify it or buy a new truck, which we could not afford at this time. We arrived at the gravel pit to load up after about three days of being beaten. When we loaded the truck, we beat Max for the first time by quite a bit. I commented about this to Jack on the way back to the worksite. Jack said that he would still beat us and had probably just slowed down a bit.

Much to our surprise Max jumped up onto the tray of the truck and started to shovel the gravel off with his giant shovel. Jack yelled out and asked why he did not use the winch. Max turned around; we had not noticed before as he had been working side on to us; Max had a huge cut from his jaw to behind his ear with lots of stitches showing. The new tipper truck's dog clutch had not dropped in, and the winch handle had caught him on the jaw as at turned wildly.

Most other people would have had their neck broken by the impact …. Max did go back to using the tipper tray but was a lot more careful when winding the tray up.

The Great White crab killer

We were looking for a different income source for our fishing venture during the closed part of the Rock Lobster fishing season. There were a lot of sand crabs in the bays nearby, so a mate and I built a lot of traps out of galvanized square mesh. The traps looked like large parrot cages. The price of sand crabs was not that great, but it was a way of utilizing our 45-foot boat, the Nancy J. After a few modifications to the traps, we were catching quite a lot of crabs on a daily basis.

One cold, still morning, we set out to pull the crab pots up. When we pulled the first pot out of the water, it looked as if it had been run over by a truck. The pot was flattened, and a hole was torn in one of the corners. My mate said, "What the hell would have done that. A bloody seal? ". Nearly all of the other traps that had been pulled had suffered the same demise. We noticed that the mesh on the pots had been scratched with something sharp, so the seal theory was not right. We returned home with hardly any crabs for our day's hard work. We set out the next day and started to pull the crab pots, only to find them in the same condition. We had spent a long time the previous day tying them up with wire and bending the mesh back straight before we could bait them up, ready for the next morning.

There had been sightings of a large Great White Shark in the bays. A guy who was a professional scallop diver had had a nasty fright when he had encountered it while diving. He had shot out of the water and had just gotten into his boat just in time. He said he had left the water so fast he had nearly overshot the boat and landed in the water on the other side of it. This curtailed his diving for a while. We reckoned that the pots had been attacked by a shark.

We set out the next morning with a small frozen tuna for bait, a huge strong hook, and some steel chain hooked to a heavy rope. We also had a .303 rifle and some bullets. I had filed the nose of the bullets down so they would act as a dumdum bullet and flatten out on impact to try and kill our prey. We also had a bucket of fish guts and blood to try to lure the shark to our boat.

We anchored the boat near where the crab pots were set and ladled some of the burley into the water. It was not a very long wait before we saw a large fin cutting through the water, coming toward our boat. I had chopped the tuna in half with a machete on the hatch cover of the boat.

My mate had loaded the rifle ready for the visitor.

The shark came right up to the boat. I had tied one end of the heavy rope to the sternpost of the boat, ready for our quarry, the guy with the rifle was ready. I lowered the tuna into the water, and the large shark took it and swam alongside the boat until it took the slack out of the rope. This pulled the shark closer to the boat; my mate shot the shark in the top of the head, then quickly reloaded and shot it again.

The shark was about sixteen feet long, and it shook the boat violently as it was dying. Finally, the shark was dead, so we put a rope around the shark's body and winched its head out of the water so we could take the hook out and then cut out the jaws, which from a shark this size was worth quite a lot of money.

We had just finished removing the jaws and the very sharp teeth and were cleaning the deck when my mate yelled. "What the hell is that coming to the boat. " He was pointing to a huge fin heading toward the boat. In all of the years I had been fishing, I had never seen a fin the size of this one.

I quickly re-baited the hook and tossed the bait into the water as the huge shark arrived at the boat. The shark took the bait and then headed away from the boat; it was towing the boat sideways, and as the rope was tied off quite a lot higher than the waterline, the boat was leaning over alarmingly. The shark quickly turned and charged the boat and came straight at me as it came out of the water over the transom of the boat. I fell over and was under the huge shark. Luckily the boat had a high transom like a wooden fence. I saw that my mate had been knocked back and the rifle had been dropped in the water.

Right next to me, as I was pinned under the shark, was the sharp machete that we had used to chop the tuna up with. I sawed at the rope, which snapped as it was under a fair amount of tension from the shark. The rope snapped, and the huge white pointer shark slipped back into the water. Boy, was I pleased to see that happen. I had visions of being gobbled up by this shark as I was not too far from the huge sharp teeth. The shark had its mouth open, and gums pushed forward as in the attack mode.

When we finally got ourselves together and had calmed down a bit, we did a bit of estimating as to the size of this huge shark. We thought it must have been about twenty-two or twenty-three feet long—more than we could handle.

The crab fishing returned to normal after this, and the diver started to dive for scallops again.

The large Shipping Buoy

When I was a lad, I spent a lot of time around the Kirton Point Jetty in Port Lincoln.

Our house was directly in front of the jetty. Mother ran tearooms and an oyster bar and took in some lodgers. Father cultivated oysters in beds near the jetty. Father would travel to coffin Bay to harvest the oysters from the sea, then bring them back to Port Lincoln to hold in the sea, so they could sell them in the shop and export to Adelaide on one of the coastal trading ships.

I spent a lot of time on the jetty fishing with my mates. A real treat was when one of the huge windjammer square-rigged sailing ships came into the jetty to tie up, ready to have grain loaded onto it to go overseas to market.

Some of these huge ships came into the jetty, unaided by the small local tugboat; this was extremely interesting to watch. The sails would be furled up by the men high in the rigging until the bare minimum of sails were still set; they would be furled as the ship got closer. When the ship finally came alongside on to the jetty. It barely touched. The mooring lines were tossed to the waiting men on the jetty to be tied off. The wind direction and strength had to be just right for this to happen. The small tugboat usually had to assist in most berthing activities.

Out from the jetty was a large buoy. This was used to moor some of these sailing ships to when there was another being loaded. This buoy saved a lot of turnaround time when the jetty was busy, as it took a lot of time for one of these ships to sail from the ballast grounds out past Boston Island, where the ships lightered the rock or sand ballast off.

One of our favorite attractions during the hot days of summer was to race the two hundred meters out to this buoy, then climb up the ropes tied to it to have a rest amongst the bird poo on top of the buoy. The buoy was covered with slime, barnacles, weed, and mussels around the waterline. The ropes were always slimy too.

After this race, we would then swim back to the jetty, washing the bird poo off as we did so. This was a really good exercise for us.

A couple of mates and I were fishing on the jetty one day when we noticed that the tugboat was unhitching the buoy. The men had a stout rope and a small buoy tied to the heavy mooring chain, which they cast off, back into the sea. The tugboat towed the buoy to the other jetty to a waiting crane on a truck.

My mates and I talked about this; we were interested in seeing the buoy lifted out of the water onto the tray of a waiting truck. We thought that we had lost our swimming platform.

A few weeks later, when I set off for school, I noticed that the buoy had returned to its usual place out from the jetty. It had been scraped down and repainted. The bottom was a red antifoul paint which most of the boats had used; the top was a shiny black with the post and marker a brilliant red.

It had been a hot day in school, with no air conditioning back then. My mates and I were keen to have a good look at our newly painted swimming platform.

We swam along next to the jetty, then sat under the end piles on one of the thick crossbeams and got our breath back; we had a good boy talk about some of the hated school teachers and the like. One of my mates had been sent to get the cane for a misdemeanor. He had six hard whacks on the bottom and proudly showed off the dark red welts. He had not been too proud of them when he had first received them, though. I think the salty water was helping take the pain out of them.

Ready, set go. We all took off as fast as we could for the buoy. I remember I had come second that day. The ropes had been removed from the buoy, we had nothing to hold on to, and we were puffed out. The new paint on the sides of the buoy was really slippery. We had no option but to swim back to the jetty slowly.

We were aware of the problems that one or another of us might have, so we all swam slowly together, stopping and treading water occasionally.

The thick beam on the bottom of the jetty was finally reached, we all realized that there may easily have been a bad accident. One of us may have drowned. We talked about having to curtail our swimming races.

I told father about this when he got home from work. He had a few words about looking before you leap but was very understanding. The next night after school, he let me row him out in the dinghy he had moored on a long mooring line at the bottom of the jetty. We had a stout length of rope which we tied to the buoys post in the middle. This was visible from the jetty.

Diving for abalone

The West Coast of South Australia is a world-renown area for abalone. Growth rates for this expensive mollusk have been measured over some years, and the waters from Cape Catastrophe to Streaky bay have some very impressive growth rates measured on tagged abalone.

The industry was regulated some years ago to prevent overfishing.

This could have decimated the industry as had happened in the St Vincent Gulf prawn industry some years ago. The prawn boats just dragged bigger and more nets until the industry became unviable. The King George Whiting industry almost suffered the same demise from trawl netting by some unscrupulous fishermen.

Weather is a big factor in Abalone diving in our local ocean and rugged coastline. Huge swells build up far down south and pound our coastline, even in calm onshore weather locally.

Dave, my sheller, and I headed to Point Drummond. There was an extremely steep road leading to a beach which was surrounded by reefs where the large Green Lip Abalone grew; in the center of the track to the beach is a heavy piece of solid steel hammered deep into the road so the four-wheel-drive towing vehicles can run out a long steel cable from a winch on the front of the Utility to tow both the four-wheel drive and the large, heavy boat filled with diving compressors: harvested abalone and a motorized shark diving cage.

The air-driven motor on the shark diving cage stopped working early in the dive. It was lifted onto the boat.

I had found a good patch of abalone, so I decided to dive without the cage. We went to the area coordinated on the GPS, and I started to dive once more. I had sent up four bags filled with large abalone to my Sheller Dave.

The water visibility had lessened when a moderate sea breeze hit. Diving in murky water made me uneasy on occasions. Today was one of those days. I had the uncanny feeling I was being watched. My sixth sense came into play, and I looked up to see a large grey shape hurtling toward me. I sucked in deep and waited for the jaws to open and grab me. The shape stopped less than a meter from me and slightly turned. It was a large bull seal. I am sure he had a smile on his face as he swam off. I was sure I could feel a squishy lump in my wetsuit near my backside.

I continued diving and was working next to a wall of rock rising from the seafloor. I felt something tug on my air hose. I looked up to see a large White Pointer shark coming toward me. I pushed myself back into a narrow crevasse in the rock wall. I could have touched the five-meter shark as it swam past me.

The shark turned and came back. This time it swam close to me and allowed me to get a better look. The lump in the rear end of my wetsuit had increased in size. I thought if I were a squid, I could have used this to make the water murky so I could escape. The shark once again came toward me. It had its jaws poking out and eyes closed in attack mode. I had my diving knife in one hand, as well as the abalone lever in the other. I was prepared to fight this monster.

I lunged forward slightly and pushed the knife deeply into the shark's nose area. The shark recoiled back. It was still circling but further away from my tight crevasse. The knife was poking out of the shark's nose area; blood was seeping from the wound. I did not venture out of my safety for some fifteen minutes. When I finally did, I slowly rose to the surface. I was diving at twenty meters. I did not want to get the bends, and I had also been diving and hiding in the water from the shark for quite a while.

As I rose slowly, I peeled all distances and up and down at almost the same time with my eyes, looking for my knife stealing visitor. I was extremely pleased when I finally climbed into the boat. When I took the wetsuit off, I did have a mess to clean up.

I did not venture diving the following day. I made sure all of the fittings and other pieces on the shark diving cage were working. The cost of a new motor was a very small price to pay for the protection offered by the cage. I had thought about a circumstance involving the shark chewing through my air hose. If this had happened, I might have been his dinner....

The Fumigated Bar Room

I had been looking for gold on a mate's farm about seventy miles away and had panned about one ounce of gold in one of the creeks on the farm. For the amount of effort and the fuel to get to the farm was about break-even, back when I did this

I called at the house to thank George for letting me have a try for gold in the creek. I showed him the spoils of the days digging and panning, he bought out a bottle of port wine, and we settled in for a bit of a drink. We fixed the government of the day and buried a few no-good politicians, and generally set the world on the right path.

The farming business was not doing too well at the time. Grain and sheep prices were low, and to top this off, there were more rabbits on the farm than sheep. The rabbits were a pest as they ate a lot of the sheep feed, and also, they got into the crops and chewed off a lot of grain.

I used to go to a lot of farms and household clearing sales. These were usually conducted when a person had sold the farm or house. It was a good time to get some cash from unwanted or unneeded goods and machinery. I remembered a sale a few months before when I had bought a large box of goods. It was full of a lot of goodies and was nearly too heavy to lift in the trailer at the time. I had sorted it out when I got home and had found quite a few boxes full of rabbit fumigation gas. The Larvicide fumigant was in small glass ampoules, which were stored in holes drilled in softwood with a cover tied on

the top, this was to try to save the glass being broken, which would not have been a good idea in a car or any other closed-in situation.

George had never heard of the glass ampoules before, so I told him how the bottle was held down the burrow with long tongs, the tongs were squeezed shut to break the bottle, the burrow was then filled in with dirt, the same action was taken on all of the other active burrows in the rabbit warren. The main aim was not to get too close to this gas as it gave one a thumping headache and blurred vision if you were to smell too much of the gas.

I offered to bring the fumigant with me and spend some time trying to get rid of a lot of Georges' rabbits if a mate could come with me and stay for a few days in the single men's accommodation on the farm, which was mainly used at shearing time. We would also have a bit of gold panning in the creeks on the farm; I offered to bring our food, as well as a couple of bottles of port wine.

I arrived at the farm with my mate Harry. Harry did a lot of odd jobs around the district to help keep the wolves from the door. He was not married as his wife had shot through with another bloke some years before.

I had made a sluice box up to try and set it up to recover more gold than the panning method. The system worked pretty well. We threw some rocks in the small stream to partially dam it up, then set the sluice at the edge of the dam. In three days, we had got about six ounces of gold which was fairly good wages in those days. I suggested to Harry that we had better keep our deal with George and give the rabbits a bit of a hurry up.

We spent the next two days digging and filling the fumigated rabbit warrens on the farm; both Harry and I had got a whiff of the Larvicide on occasions when the wind had blown the gas out of the burrow we were filling in. We soon learned to start downwind with the fumigant then work our way around the burrows. The headache was almost always accompanied by a purple haze that lasted for a while. The session on the port most nights helped it to go away.

We left Georges's farm on a Friday afternoon and were driving home when we saw some cars outside a bush pub which sat with about two other houses on the side of the road. Harry suggested that we should check it out for a drink as we had a bit of time up our sleeve.

I pulled into the pub, then we walked in and ordered two beers. There was a plain-looking girl working behind the bar serving the twenty-plus patrons. We had another beer each when the girl was called back to the kitchen to help with the meals. A guy came out and started to serve behind the bar. Harry said." That's the rotten cow who took my missus. "he stormed over to the bar and started to argue with the barman. He offered to take him outside and belt the daylights out of him. The barman would have been no match for Harry as Harry was known for being very strong.

Some of the locals were getting stroppy and yelled for Harry to sit down. I could sense that there was going to be a brawl. I was not very keen on taking on the rest of the bar on Harry's account, we both would have got hiding, and I could see it getting closer by the second. I grabbed Harry and dragged him out of the bar; He was protesting loudly. I told him to shut up and get in the truck.

I was just about to drive off in the truck when I had an idea; Harry had calmed down a bit but was still grumbling about the barman. "Do you want me to stitch them up? "I asked, "bloody oath, "Said Harry. "How are you going to do that? "Just shut up and watch, "I said. I got one of the few remaining ampoules of Larvicide out of the wooden carrying container, then got out of the truck and calmly walked over to the bar of the pub; I had the small bottle in my pocket. I skirted the crowd then went to the men's toilet; I walked out of the toilet with the small bottle in my hand. I dropped the bottle behind the crowd at the bar, then calmly walked out and got in the truck.

We waited for about five minutes before some unsuspecting patron stepped on the ampoule and broke it. There was a lot of noise coming from the bar and a lot of cursing. The door was not wide enough to accommodate the mob trying to get out; there was a lot of yelling and pushing until all of the men and women were out on the lawn.

As I slowly drove off in the truck, I could see the people pulling tufts of lawn grass up and rubbing their sore eyes with it to get the stinging gas out. I bet there were some purple headaches as they all left for home.

I have driven past this small hotel on many occasions but have never returned for a beer in case the Barman or one of the patrons might have a long memory.

The magnificent oyster

Father used to travel to Coffin Bay on a regular basis to buy oysters from the oyster fishermen, who were dredging the bay for the succulent oysters. He also took the Chrysler buckboard with the oversized tires to Yangi and other out-of-the-way places to get them himself. I used to love going to help.

Father would drive the Chrysler buckboard down as close as he could to the water near the Kirton point Jetty to unload them and put them into the wire netting baskets to wait for transport or some to be sold locally.   The oysters were sold in the shop as a meal or in dozen lots. There was a good demand for Coffin Bay oysters at the time.

When the oysters were sold to Adelaide or even Melbourne, they were put into wheat bags. There was a method of packing them. First, a layer of seaweed off the beach, then a layer of oysters, then seaweed again; this was repeated until the bag was filled. Then the bag was sewn up with a needle and twine. The seaweed in the bags kept the oysters moist and cool.

Father was in the shop one day when a visitor to a town called in. Father had looked him over and had concluded that he looked a bit of a smart ass.

The smart tourist commented on an oyster which father had just shucked and put into a jar; he was going to cook this huge oyster for tea. The smart tourist commented about the size of this oyster. Father, in his dry wit, offered the tourist five pounds if he could eat this oyster and keep it down. The smarty said, "You are on. I have come into the shop for a feed of oysters; this will be the easiest five pounds I have ever earned. Five pounds were about three weeks' wages at that time—a lot of money. The smart tourist took the oyster out of the jar and, with about four chews, swallowed it down. "Where is my money, "he asked father. Father asked him if he really felt OK. "Of course I am Ok, now give me my money." Father peered at the man and waited for a short while. the man was getting a bit agitated. "You know a man came into the shop just before you, and he ate that oyster and chucked up all over the floor of the shop. His dog picked the oyster up and ran outside, and he ate it also. None of them could keep it down. I thought you would have trouble too". Father said it was good wages to clean the mess off the floor of the shop. The guy paid the money but was extremely angry. He threatened to get the police and health department.

A Labrador Retriever

It was Friday night. Work had been challenging all week with a major breakdown in the plant. One guy knew all about fixing this problem. What a mess it took us an extra day to fix his stuff up.

I was at the Tasman hotel with some mates grizzling about the lost production and the mess we had to clean up.

One of my mates suggested a fishing trip could be a good game changer and get me to relax again. "There are some schools of Tuna outside of Williams Island heading toward the Neptune's" This pricked my ears up as Tuna were a nice addition to the diet. I had a large smokebox and liked to have smoked tuna on hand also.

Three guys volunteered to come with me in my forty-foot diesel fast boat.

"You can bring your wives as well. The weather is pretty good. They can have a mag and then maybe catch a fish. We can all sleepover at Memory Cove."

We were to meet at the wharf at ten o'clock in the morning.

I drove down to the wharf after getting some booze and food. The guys and their wives were waiting.

I usually took our Black Labrador Retriever with me on the boat. I had Blackie with me. She bounded out of the car and gave all the customary lick, then waited to be lifted down into the boat.

It was a magnificent day. I had the boat running at twenty knots heading south. On the way, we had sandwiches the women were making for lunch.

We arrived at the fishing grounds at two-thirty and spied a group of birds working a school of fish. As we came closer, we could see the tuna breaking the water as they chased the school of pilchards and ate them.

During the afternoon, we caught six plump tuna weighing between ten and twenty kilograms.

My wife caught the larges one, which was a bit of a let-down to be shown up by a woman when you had mates nearby.

I also thought about having a look in the small sheltered bay on Williams Island on the way back to Memory Cove. This sometimes had some schools of trevally or salmon swimming there.

We entered the small bay and noticed that there were some salmon schools swimming around there.

I went down below and came back with a stick of Gelignite with a detonator and fuse fitted.

"How about getting a couple of large dab nets from the rear locker," I asked the men.

"Hey, that's pretty illegal to blow up fish with dynamite," one guy said. " There is no one else around, so I'll take a chance" The men had the long-handled dab nets ready.

I had Blackie standing next to me at the time. I lit the fuse of the Gelignite and tossed it into the ocean. Blackie pushed past me and then dove into the water and grabbed the gelignite before it sank down and then swam back to the boat.

The fuse was not very long on the plug of gelignite. As she was at the boat, I ripped it out of her mouth and tossed it as far as I could. Boom. The gelignite exploded in midair.

I reached down and grabbed blackie's collar. I towed her over the transom of the boat and dumped her on the deck.

There was a deathly silence among my guests and wife at the time. I went and started to boat motor and headed for Memory Cove

If the gelignite had exploded next to the boat hull, it would have blown a large hole through the fiberglass. The shards of this blown off could have killed us all.

The Opal Thieves

It was in the mid-nineteen seventies. I had a few weeks in between jobs; I went to go and stay y with a friend at Coober Pedy to have a look around.

At this time, there was a rush on at Coober Pedy. A new field had been discovered; there were about two and a half thousand miners working around this field. There was the old Yorke hoist, which was pulling the dirt and rock in a bucket, the new blower's, which sucked the dirt out through a pipe, similar to a large vacuum cleaner, and bulldozers on the shallow areas. About one hundred and fifty dozers were working. The day after I arrived at Coober Pedy, I visited the Mines Department and obtained a permit to peg a claim. I then went to the Miners Store and bought four wooden posts to peg a claim with. I had to wait for the tags that had to be nailed onto the posts for two days to come up from Adelaide.

I drove the old utility out to the Fourteen Mile Field to have a look around. This place was a sea of activity. Small iron houses had been hastily built in groups away from the main workings. Each claim had some vehicles parked on it. Men were walking around doing jobs or pulling dirt that had been mined deep below the surface.

Dust was blowing out of the blowers as they sucked the dirt and rocks into a hopper, which dropped the dirt into heaps. Small and large drills were either drilling holes or parked on the claims waiting.

I had passed a lot of bulldozers working the shallow ground as I had driven into the main area. Finally, I came to the end of the hundreds of mining pegs that denoted each claim. The flat ground was covered in small bushes; some had pretty flowers on them.

The next morning, I obtained my tags to put on my posts. I returned to the field and headed past the last claims, and put my posts in. I measured the distances with a fifty-meter tape I had borrowed from my mate. I then took the coordinates from the Mines Department survey peg with a compass then measured all of the coordinates of each corner post with the compass. This was all written down on a piece of paper.

The woman in the Mines Department office recorded all of the details on a form then gave me some numbers to write on the pegs to say the claim was registered.

I bought some lunch from the service station then headed back to paint the numbers on the pegs. As I drove to the claim, I noticed that one of the large Caldwell drills was drilling on a claim nearby. When they had finished, I walked across and asked if they would drill a hole for me. The driller's name was Don, he was Italian, and he agreed to drill a hole for five hundred dollars to the fifty-foot depth the opal was in this area.

The drill was moved to my claim.

I picked a place for the drill to work in the middle of the claim. The stabilizing legs were pulled out. The drill leveled up, and then the tall mast was raised. The Kelly bar and bucket were lowered to the ground. The bucket started to turn and dig.

A rope and a wire hawser had to be attached to the bucket top each time it was pulled out of the ground. The hawser would pull the bucket and Kelly bar sideways from the hole; the rope was then pulled to drop the hinged bottom of the bucket to let it drop and empty the dirt. The same procedure was carried out many times. The Kelly bar and bucket crunched through something solid. When the bucket was pulled, the heap was covered with dazzling opal stones. We all had sieves and sieved the opal from the dirt. I had a bucket in the utility; we tossed all of the opals into this bucket. I did notice that the odd piece did go into one of the guy's pockets. I did not want a fight on the field with three desperadoes, so I kept my mouth shut.

Another bucket of dirt was taken out; then, I was lowered down into the hole with a bucket, light, and small pick. The opal circled the hole. I had a good find of opal, worth a lot of money. I dug all of the loose pieces of opal out. I was then pulled out of the hole.

I drove back to Coober Pedy and told my mate, who had just returned from mining. I showed him the opal. He estimated that there was fifteen thousand dollars worth of opal in the bucket.

We went to where he was working and picked up his Yorke hoist and tools from his claim. He was not finding opal very much at this time. We were ready to get working the next morning.

When we arrived to work the next morning, the claim had pegs all around the three unpegged sides. The Italian guy's drill was drilling on our boundary. Another drill was drilling on the claim I had pegged next to. A man in a uniform was measuring the coordinates of the claim. I asked what he was doing. I was informed that some person had plain ted my claim. Therefore we were not allowed to work until the matter had been to court in two months' time.

Evidently, some person had said that I had made a mistake with the measurements of the claim. I asked who. The mine warden said he was not allowed to divulge this. My friend asked if it were one of the persons drilling next to our border, the mines warden was not going to say. The conversation had gotten pretty heated.

I had been in a hurry to get a shaft drilled in my claim and had asked one of the most dishonest crooks in town to do it. Don was not a nice man, nor were his brothers and the men who worked for him. The other drill working on the other boundary belonged to a group of Serbians who were of the same ilk.

We knew exactly what the drills were drilling for. It was to allow them access to our opal. The mines warden was evidently in on the act for a percentage.

I did suggest to my mate that we blow the drills up. Peter had no desire to take on the Coober Pedy mafia and a mob of mad Serbs.

The court case resolved the matter in my favor. I had come back for the case. Peter and I went to the claim. He lowered me down on his hoist on his truck. There were two drives leading from the claims, which had the drills on them. A huge ballroom had been dug under the hole I had dug.

I went to the police. They were not interested. I went to the Mines Department and found the guy who had put the plaint notice on my claim. He told me to put it down to a bad experience.

The Stolen Fish

The weather had been perfect for the last three days: nice warm days and still nights. I had phoned my brother-in-law Jack and Keith and suggested that we go to Coffin Bay to see if we could spear some flounder to top our larders up.

I picked the men up about five o'clock in fathers Chrysler buckboard. The buckboard had been modified, having larger rims and truck tyres fitted so we could go through the sand hills at Coffin Bay to get the oysters we sold in our shop and sent away on the coastal trading ship the Minnipa to be sold in Adelaide.

We had a can of kerosene for the flares and a heap of flares made up to see the fish in the shallow water. As we drove along the bumpy road, we talked about the fishing trips we had been on before.

One of the night's trips was nearly a disaster as we had not left a light or fire on the beach where the buckboard was parked. All we had was the kerosene flares, which just showed a small area in which we were fishing. We had walked a long way chasing the elusive flounders, not realizing that we were in the middle of the bay. We had followed the edge of the channel and had been spearing the fish as we went. This night was very dark with no moon, and as we went to return to the Buckboard, we got lost. In front of us was a deep channel; the tide was also coming in, luckily we had plenty of kerosene for the flares.   After about half an hour, we finally hit the beach. We had started to navigate by the stars, crossing some deep water up to our necks. Where was the buckboard on the long beach? As luck would have it, we walked in the right direction. Boy, were we happy to see the dim out- line of the buckboard as we neared it? One learns from one's mistakes, hopefully. As we arrived at Coffin Bay, we pulled off the road into the scrub on the edge of the beach. We searched around for some wood to make a beacon fire, also somewhere to dry off and have a swig out of the wine flagon we had bought with us.

What a beautiful night, there was plenty of fish, flounder on the bottom, They were usually only distinguished by the two black eyes, as the flounder was a master of disguise, there were also some nice flathead, some very large, the occasional whiting and some garfish which were netted with a dab-net.

Each of us had a gunnysack, a sugar bag with a rope tied to one top corner and one bottom corner, and the fish were stowed in this. When a garfish was spotted, Jack would come across with the dab net and catch it.

We worked our way back to the glowing embers of our fire. We were extremely happy about the good night's fishing and were looking forward to a long swig of Port Wine out of the waiting flagon.   Keith got the large fish basket out of the tray of the buckboard. We tipped our fish into it and then had a couple of swigs of wine each. Keith, who had always been a bit hungry, suggested that we go and get some more fish, as there were evidently plenty more out there. We reluctantly agreed as the night was getting a bit cold by now. We lit the flares and started out looking for the fish. We must have walked miles for about four fish, and the tide must have changed or something. Keith was the first to start to grumble about the fish; Jack and I reminded him that it had been his idea.

When we finally arrived back at the fire, we found that the fishing basket was missing, and someone had also drunk the rest of the flagon of port wine.

There was much cursing by all and what we would do if we were lucky enough to find the mongrels which had stolen our fish.

There is a post script to this story.

I was in the hospital for a few days, sixty-five years later. In the next bed was a guy who I had worked with on occasions when I was plumbing. He was a bricklayer by the name of Ted. We were reminiscing about the good old days: truck driving, spotlighting, and fishing trips. Tom mentioned one of his good fishing trips at Coffin Bay.

Tom and a mate were doing a bit of building work at Coffin Bay, and on the way home, after they had imbibed on some wine with the guy who they were working for. They had noticed the fire not far off the road and had seen the fish basket. They had stolen the big basket filled with fish and had found a half flagon of wine and had drunk that too. I could not help myself. "You rotten bastard, I always thought of you as a friend. You are the mongrel who stole our fish". I did not feel like laughing at this one-off, even after all of these years.

One of my best mates and father-in-law's fascinating stories is John Henry Ives.

Dr. Trudie and the shark

The day was warm with a bit of a lazy north wind. I had been driving on a lot worse days than this. We Had picked up a load of charcoal just out from port Lincoln at the Duck Ponds. There were quite a few old dead red gums in the area, which were dragged and put into a pit to make the charcoal. The pit was covered with rusty roofing iron or some other medium that would not burn after the fire was lit to exclude the air to make the charcoal. The charcoal work was pretty dirty as the dust tended to stick and paint one's body black.

Along the way, there were other heaps of bagged charcoal that were sold on the honesty method of putting the money into a locked steel box or some other sort of device. If one was found to leave without paying, there was usually hell to pay if the perpetrator was found out. On a good day, we could get to Elliston on three to four fills of charcoal, which in itself was dirty work. The real dirty work was if one of the large flock filled filters were to block up, the truck would consistently lose power which was occurring today

I was driving by myself today, so I could not share the soot with a mate, which was a pity I had quite a few drop-offs on the way, mainly boxes of power kerosene for the tractors of the time. Each box had two four-gallon tins inside; I did manage to have a bit of cleanup at one of the farmer's sheds, at the tank by the windmill.

I arrived at Elliston about five o'clock in the afternoon. The clouds had been building up all day, and it was starting to look a bit thundery.

This was usually a good time to go and get a feed of salmon at the Salmon Hole at Elliston. I had finished unloading the Elliston freight and had adjourned to the pub to stay the night.

The Elliston pub had certain spots where the regular drinkers stood, as did a lot of bush pubs.

Dock Trudy was in his usual spot at the hotel bar. Ah, the plumber, he used to call me as I had been plumbing before the war. We had a couple of drinks when Trudy suggested to the bar that we should get over to the Salmon Hole to get a feed of fish. All Agreed.

One of the guys had a three-ton Bedford truck, so he offered to drive. There were about six guys and three nurses from the hospital who elected to go. We hunted around and got some flares and some kerosene. Trudy had his old fishing kit bag.

We clambered down the jagged rocks in the weak moonlight to the more jagged rocks around the salmon hole. We lit a flare and noticed a large school of salmon swimming in the hole. The limestone ringed hole was about fifty meters across and had a shallow entrance leading to it through the reef about five meters wide.

Trudy got his kit bag and took a weeping old-looking stick of gelignite, pushed a fuse and detonator into the jelly, then lit the fuse and tossed it into the hole among the fish. Whoomph there was water over everyone when the flares were lit again there was also a lot of salmon lying stunned on top of the water. "Right Let's get the fish. "He clambered into the water. One of the guys yelled for him to get out as there was about an eight to nine-foot white pointer shark, which had just slid over the rocks into the entrance of the salmon hole." Shark! Get out, Trudy. He will get you. "Trudy, who was only dressed in a pair of shorts and had sandshoes on his feet, yelled back. " This rotter is not going to get my fish; he won't hurt you; come and help." trudge was tossing the stunned salmon up onto the rocks and pushing the shark out of the way with his sandshoe shod foot cursing us for being so lazy. Needless to say, the shark did not get Trudy, but none of us were prepared to take a chance. The next morning, I was just getting into the truck to continue on to Streaky Bay when one of the nurses who had been with our fishing. She walked to the truck and asked me to call and see the Doctor before I left town.

We had taken a few bottles of wine down to the salmon hole. They evidently had not given us any nerve as far as the shark was concerned, but they had given us a bad hangover, especially Trudy, who had been in fine form on the way back to town.

I walked over toward the Hospital and noticed Trudy sitting on the steps of his house". "Ah, the plumber, come inside and have a look. I had a bit of a problem last night with a bloody blowfly in my room. "I followed Trudy into his room and noticed a hole in the Wunderlich patterned steel ceiling. "what happened, Trudy? "I asked. "I could not catch this bloody blowfly last night; The damned ceilings are too high; I shot the bastard with the twelve-gauge shotgun. "

'Hell", I said that must have rattled things up a bit," I don't know about rattling, but my ears were ringing for a while. "

I walked back to the truck and drove to a friend's house and got a couple of offcuts from some roofing iron and went back and fixed the roof and patched the ceiling from the top before I nailed the new iron down, the repair is probably still there if the house is still standing.

Dr. Trudinger was a brilliant surgeon when sober. He was sometimes fed some special pills to sober him up when an emergency happened. A traveling salesman for a grocery company had a burst appendix and was in a very poor condition in hospital one day. While waiting for the doctor to attend him, he was accosted by a man very inebriated. He rang the matron of the hospital with the bedside bell. He was told the drunk was the doctor giving him his pre-op examination. The guy survived. He would not have if he were not operated on.

Red Hot Willie

Our first farm was in the Sheringa district near Elliston in South Australia; by district standards, it was very small at seven and a half thousand acres. We could only run around thirteen hundred sheep on this property. And put a small area of crop in. This was usually shared farmed by the kangaroos and the destructive emus. The main problem with the Sheringa district was not the rainfall, and this was quite good. It was the lack of soil. There were huge areas of sheet hard limestone rock.

We had three blocks of land that were separated by neighbors. We had about two thousand acres in the home block and seven hundred acres in a block called Manu. Then about ten miles from home was a block called East End. East End was a sort of heath country which was deficient in some minerals and did not grow much feed. I had tried some plots with different trace elements to no avail. There was a bit over four thousand acres on this block; there were about five hundred acres of beautiful straight trunked red gum trees growing there. We ran about three hundred old weathers on this part of the property. Under the limestone, there was excellent water; there were fourteen windmills scattered over the property, mainly on shallow wells with a stone tank and trough. The sheep drank from these troughs, as well as the abundance of kangaroos and emus.

My father-in-law John Henry and Jean, the Mother in law came to visit on a Saturday and were going to stay the weekend. I was really looking forward to the visit as I really liked John Henry. He was one of those blokes who had done a lot of different things in his life and was keen on fishing, as was I. He had also driven trucks during the war in and around the area and knew a lot of interesting stories. On Saturday, I took Johnnie out to check to see if all of the windmills were working and cleaning out the troughs. I was also looking for a fresh kangaroo to go into the dog's fridge for dog food. As we traveled from one windmill to another, the day heated up. We had been keeping our eye out for a kangaroo but had not seen any. We left Manu and headed out through Kappawanta Station toward East End. This was usually the place where a kangaroo would be lying under some mallee or red gum trees.

I was driving an International Scout utility. A small four-wheel drive. The Scout had the same sort of windows as a Land Rover, the two-piece sliding window. I did not like them as if you wanted to shoot a fox or a kangaroo; the door had to be opened to allow you to sight the gun; when the door was opened, it always made a loud clanging noise, and the animals usually bolted. The other way was to lean right back in the cabin and just have the end of the rifle barrel out the small window.

This did work OK. I had an automatic twenty-two caliber rifle and had become a fairly good shot. We were halfway between the bottom and top windmill when Johnnie said softly. "There is a Kangaroo laying

under that bush." I stopped the utility and leaned back in the cab, and fired the shot. I hit the animal in the head and killed the kangaroo.

  Johnnie let out a yell, "hell, have you got bees out here; something has bitten me. "He jumped out of the utility. There were bees at the windmill we were traveling to, so I thought he must have been stung. He was jumping around, trying to get his shorts and undies off. He finally succeeded. On the end of his pointy bit was the bullet shell stuck fast. "What will I do now? It's really stuck ". "Don't look at me. I am not into that sort of thing; this looks like your problem. "was my answer. After about two minutes of spitting on his fingers and getting the shell wet, he finally had the shell off. He had a very red T-shaped brand on the head of his large donger. He very carefully dressed and gingerly sat on the seat for the trip to the next mill.

The bullet shell had ejected out of the breech of the gun and ricochet off the window up the leg of his shorts; it had been red hot. When we arrived home, he got some sunburn cream and gave the offending member a good smear to take the heat out of it.

The Giant Stingray

I had had a fall off a ladder while building a new shed on our farm. I had already built two sheds by myself and a large one with help from a couple of mates. The fourth one bought my demise. I remember falling and possibly doing a summersault in the air from the fifteen-foot ladder. I had a lad helping me at this time.

I came too, laying on the ground; I thought of how lucky I was not to have hurt myself, this was until I tried to rise up and my busted leg gave out. This was extremely painful. I was taken by air ambulance from the Tumby Bay hospital. The local ambulance had taken me there. Glenys traveled to Adelaide on the plane. I spent many hours in Adelaide. I left the hospital with rings around my leg and bolts through the bones of my leg. So much for a simple broken leg. Mine had exploded on impact with the ground.

Months of sitting around reading and writing were driving me crazy.

I was getting very adept on crutches.

The mate who helped build the previous shed called and asked if I would like a day trip on his brother's prawn boat. They were going out in Boston Bay to test some new prawn nets they had made. I had to be winched down onto the boat. At least I was out on the sea again.

The aim of the test was to drop the nets and trawl for five minutes

, then pull the trawl in and weigh the catch. The first pull showed a large discrepancy in the weight of the bycatch and prawns caught.

There was a mixed bag of fish and shellfish when the trawls were raised. There were Flathead, flounder, salmon trout scallops, oysters, and quite a few large prawns. The last lift of the trawl was tipping the large boat to one side as the trawl was being winched aboard. I thought they must have hooked onto an old wrecked boat or someone's favorite snapper spot with an old car body as a shelter for the fish. As the net was pulled over to the sorting table, there was a giant stingray caught inside.

 When the net was emptied onto the sorting table, one of the crew ran to the rear of the stingray and cut off its tail with a machete. The tail was over a meter long It had a poisonous barb about fourteen or fifteen centimeters long

The reason for removing the tail was for the crew's safety in trying to move the seven or eight-hundred-kilogram fish from the table. One slash with this barb could have incurred a very nasty wound. We had to sit on the boat and eat all of the freshly cooked prawns, as we were not allowed to take the prawns from testing of the boat

Uncles Claude's Big Nuts

I had been invited to go fishing with Uncle Claude. I really liked our fishing trip as my uncle had done a lot of different things in his life. He always seemed to have a new and interesting story to tell while we were waiting for a fish to bite.

We always went to Farm Beach, a bay where if the wind were to change to the west, getting the boat out was a bit difficult. These westerly wind changes did not happen very often; today was an exception; the wind had changed and was blowing about ten knots. This was a disappointment as the fishing had really been good. We had a nice assortment of different types of fish; they were still biting.

As we headed toward the beach in uncle's small fiberglass boat, he explained how he would jump over the side to steady the boat when we hit the shore. We could see in the distance that there was a bit of wash coming up the beach as the waves broke.

We were nearly at the beach when uncle stood up, ready to jump overboard to assist in holding the boat. He was wearing a pair of fairly long shorts that day, as was I. Just before the beach, a wave came and lifted the stern of the boat. I was driving at the time and had cut the motor and lifted it onto the chock so the propeller would not get damaged.

The next thing I saw was uncle going head first over the bow of the boat, his shorts got hooked into the anchor bollard, and his face was in the sand. The offending wave had receded, leaving the boat high and dry. Uncle Claude was very quiet, as I presumed he had a mouth full of sand, a bit unusual for Uncle.

The thick denim shorts were holding him, stopping him from getting up on his feet. I opened the fishing box and got the rusty fishing knife out, and started to cut his shorts through. Uncle Claude let out a scream like a charging bull elephant; I stopped cutting." What's wrong? "I asked with a bit of concern. "You are cutting my skin, you stupid cow." I had not noticed the blood; I did now it was flowing freely.

I jumped over the side of the boat and tried to lift him; he was a big man; I finally got his shorts unhooked and found his testicles hooked on the bollard. I heaved on the side of the boat, and they popped free. Uncle said a few nasty things before he finally calmed down. I got his handkerchief and tied a knot in it around the bleeding part of his anatomy. By this time, he had apologized for the nasty remarks.   Uncle sat on the beach while I got the old Land Rover and boat trailer backed into the boat. I winched the boat on the trailer and headed for home. As we traveled home, I asked uncle if he had forgotten to put his undies on that morning. Uncle replied that he had never worn undies; they had always squeezed his large testicles, making it hard to walk.   We arrived home at about five o clock and went to the hospital first,

One of the nurses had a look at uncle's problem and then called the local doctor in. she was having trouble not to laugh when she heard the full story. Claude was not too amused about this. I had done a pretty good job of cutting the shorts; I had nearly made uncle a soprano. The doctor arrived and checked the damage. Luckily for Claude, the only part cut was the skin, not the important bits inside. It took six stitches to seal the damage that I had done.

"Aside from the damage, Claude did you catch any fish?" asked the doctor "we got a fair few," said Claude. "I reckon you nearly got your bag limit," said the doctor.

Aunty had a good laugh when I finally got Claude home. He was not very amused at some of the comments she said about the near-castration event.

The oval curator

Some years ago, a mate was looking after an oval in an inland Australian town

Kev had opened his mouth again at a meeting of the local football club and had offered to water and mow the local oval

This job was quite rewarding except for the damage the hordes of cockatoos did when feeding on the sweet green grass.

I would go to the oval to shift the sprinkler system to another area, and there was always about two hundred Galah's feeding on the grass. One huge problem was that they were not only feeding but pulling the lawn up to get at the sweet roots on the bottom. These destructive birds were also killing some of the gum trees planted around the perimeter of the car park. The rotten sods would chew all of the new shoots off the trees, then do the same to the new shoots that replaced the chewed-off ones.

I had tried different measures like steel posts with silver-paper scares tied to flutter in the wind. These all worked for about two or three days; then, the birds took no notice of them.

I arrived one morning with a pocket filled with shotgun shells and my pride and joy the double barrel shotgun. The birds were packed together, feeding in a mob. There were no houses on the other side of the oval, just the edge of the saltbush plain. I aimed at the mob then pulled the trigger. As the bids rose together, I fired into the mass of flying birds.

A dense cloud of grey and pink feathers floated off in the wind. Underneath this, there were about ten Galahs unable to fly. I dispatched these with a stick I carried for the job. I picked the birds up by putting them into a plastic bag, ready to travel home. The next day the birds were missing. Within three days, they were back feeding again. I gave them the same treatment and removed another five of the pests. As I was packing the hoses up, a police car entered the oval; the car drove over to where I was working.

A tired-looking policeman got out of the car and walked over to me.

"We have had a complaint about you shooting Galahs on the oval, "Who dubbed me in. "I asked. "I can't tell you that," The cop said. I will let you fire over the head of the Galahs to scare them".

The next two days were galah-free. They returned with some extra mates and set about destroying the lawn grass again. I fired one barrel of shot over their heads; just as they took to flight, I let the other barrel go and took out another four birds.

The tired cop arrived as I was packing up again. This time he was getting nasty. "Been killing galah's again, I see. If I catch you shooting galah's again, I will confiscate your gun". I would like to know who is dubbing me all of the time. Is it the old guy with the palm tree in the front yard?" The cop looked across to the house. I was now sure I had found the culprit. This guy and his wife were always feeding the Galahs and other birds with oats. They laid a trail alongside the road in front of their house at least once a week.

On the way home, that night I called at the local hardware store and bought a large box of poisoned grain used for poisoning rats. Later that night, when it was nice and dark, I drove toward the oval; I took the large box of poison. I parked well away from the oval and walked to the street in front of my bird-feeding maniac with the palm tree in the yard.

My eyes had grown accustomed to the dark. I removed the lid from the poison and tipped the grain out as I walked along where they fed the birds.

The tired cop arrived as I was setting up to do the watering. He was pretty angry. "There are about fifty dead birds lying in the street next to the oval. Have you been poisoning those birds now"?" Of course, not," Well, who laid all of the grain across the street. "The old coot in the house with the palm tree out front usually feeds the birds," The cop drove off and stopped out front of the house with the large palm tree in front. I could hear him and the crazy bird feeding old mongrel having a heated discussion.

Dr Trudinger kit bag

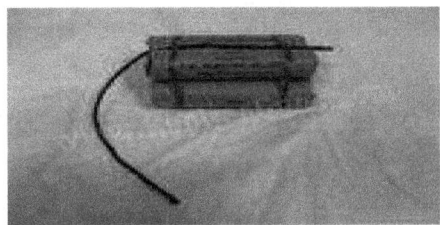

The local Fishing Inspector was staying at the Elliston Hotel to check up on the local fishermen to see that no rules were being broken. The stay was a stop in a week's work to travel from Port Lincoln to Ceduna. He was on his way back to Port Lincoln.

The Inspector was not averse to a wee drink occasionally. He started talking to the local doctor Doc Trudy. Dr. Trudinger was a local legend who had saved a lot of lives in the district. He was a brilliant surgeon. There was only one problem; before he could operate, he had to take two white pills to sober himself up.

Trudy offered to take the inspector out in his dinghy to check the bay. Trudy had a thirteen-foot plank dinghy with a three-horse-powered Seagull outboard motor on the rear.

In their trip around the bay, Trudy noticed a dark patch under the boat. On further inspection, it was found to be a large school of salmon. The boat was throttled back and turned back over this big school of fish. Trudy rummaged around under the rear seat of the boat and pulled out an old kit bag. In amongst the fishing lines, hooks and sinkers were three weeping sticks of gelignite. Trudy deftly pushed the detonator and short fuse into the end of the explosive. The Fishing inspector protested, "Hey, you should know that is illegal. You will get a hefty fine if you try to blow fish up with explosives. If you toss that gelignite in amongst the fish, I will take you to court." Trudy smiled at the inspector, lit the fuse, and then said," I do not think I will toss the explosives into the water, my boy. I think you will. "Trudy tossed the now lit stick of gelignite to the Fishing Inspector, who quickly tossed it over the side of the boat. He was not too proud to take an illegal feed of fish home with him when he left.

The Opal Turtles

Nick the Greek disappeared toward the bar. Nick had a real history in Coober Pedy. As he, like some Greeks tend to be, he was a rather shady character. When a rush was on in a new field, nick used to hire a bus in Adelaide and fill it with friends and acquaintances to come to Coober Pedy to peg claims in the new field. Nick offered them ten percent of all opal found. Needless to say that most of them had a trip to Coober Pedy and a good look around and saw no money. An occasional good-looking woman was asked back to help on her claim. Nicky usually had ulterior motives.

Nick had a beautiful Greek wife and four kids in Adelaide who knew what he was like and was not very pleased.

Nick made two trips through the crowd with the drinks. He sat at the table. "Did I ever tell you about the first shaft I dug at Coober Pedy in nineteen sixty-one? I pegged a claim and dug it down by hand. I climbed up and fished for the buckets of dirt, which I stacked three high in the shaft. These were twenty-liter buckets with handles; I climbed past the buckets out of the shaft then used the hook on the steel cable on the windlass to fish for each bucket handle to pull it out. I held a mirror and shined the reflection down the shaft so I could see. I had had plenty fishing experience at Port Kenny when I was a kid." Nick emptied his glass of beer.

"I get you another round. Nick waddled through the crowd again and returned with the glasses". The women had only started to drink the white wine.

I hit the bottom of the shaft and could not dig anymore. It is like I am trying to dig through the glass. I have only a candle for light. I get the candle and sweep the loose dirt off the floor of the shaft with my hand. Bloody hell, it is thick opal. I have to go back to town and buy a heavy hammer and chisel to dig a hole in the opal so I can start to prize it out". Nick took a long drink of beer. "I get the opal out, then I dig and find a full opal tortoise more than two feet long. I dig him out. He will not fit in the bucket.

I leave him there and go to town and ask a mate of mine. He tells me that the government will take this from you as it is a fossil. I went back then broke the tortoise up with the hammer. I find two more tortoises and break them too. I would like to find that mate now. I found out later that these tortoises would have been worth five hundred thousand pounds each. I did find two hundred and eighty thousand pounds the first year. A car was four hundred pounds, and a reasonable house was a thousand pounds. I turned one and a half million into fifteen thousand. Bloody bastard cost me all of that money".

I have heard a Coober Pedy Greek tell another story of the hole Nick dug. Nick had a young Greek as a partner. The lad's job was to wind the dirt out of the hole with the windlass. Nick did not offer him the chance to check to see if there were any opal.

When Nick found the opal in the floor of the hole, he had come out of the hole and had sworn and tossed his beanie to the ground. "All that bloody work for nothing. We have gone past where the opal should be by ten feet. The bloody neighbors must have gotten all the opals and left us none. I feel sorry for you, boy doing all of the work. Here take the twenty pounds to buy some food." Nick had then reached into his pocket and gave the lad the twenty pounds

He drove the lad back to town, then bought the hammer and chisel to dig the opal out.

Duck-shot Bum

During my travels around our part of the world, I have met some interesting characters; one such person was Tom.

Tom was a Yorkshire boy who had been sent out to Australia after the war, Tom and his wife ran a farm.

Tom was a very interesting man to talk to. He always has a yarn about something interesting. I always liked to hear the next story when we occasionally met.

The main bitumen highway ran past Tom's house, which was about one hundred meters from the road. The first thing one noticed was that there were always a lot of chickens and ducks running alongside the main road.

There would have been good pickings for grain during harvest time, as some of the grain trucks traveling back and forth to town would leak a small amount of grain. Also, when there was enough rain to run off the bitumen, there would be a bit of green feed coming up.

I was talking to Tom one day and then mentioned the poultry running on the road and asked if there were many skittled by the cars and trucks. Tom said that he occasionally found a flattened bird that had met its demise but not too many as most seemed to be wise to the traffic. "I do have a good story about this, though." This was always a good lead into a good yarn.

"Every bloody Sunday at about one-thirty in the afternoon, a white Zephyr car would pull up on the edge of the road, and a guy would get out and chase some of my ducks along the netting fence by the road. He had a long piece of fencing wire with a hook on end, which he would use to hook the legs of one of my ducks. He always caught three ducks before leaving".

Tom paused the story, got his tobacco out of his pocket, and then rolled a cigarette; he lit the smoke then resumed the tale.

"I was not too happy with this guy taking the poultry and decided to wait to see if he returned the next week as he had for the last four. I had a talk with my wife about this, and I decided to sit on the miner's couch on the front veranda of the house with my trusty four ten shotgun, which we kept around the house in the summer in case of a snake hanging around,".

Tom stubbed his cigarette out and resumed the tale.

"The white Zephyr was right on time. The car stopped, and the guy got out with his trusty piece of wire and caught the first duck; he had tied the bird's legs with some string before the second chase.

After a bit of a run he caught the second victim and was bending down to remove the ducks leg from the wire, he was about a hundred meters from me with his backside straight toward me. I lifted the snake gun up and pulled the trigger. I was unsure whether the small shotgun would even reach this distance. Evidently, it did as the snake stealing my ducks dropped the duck and snapped into an upright position. I had never seen anyone rise up so quickly in my life. He limped back to his white Zephyr car and very gingerly slid into the seat. The engine started, then the car slowly drove off ".

Tom got his tobacco and rolled another cigarette, then lit it; after the first puff, he resumed the story.

'My wife had been watching out the lounge room window as the duck thief had met his waterloo and was chuckling as I went inside. I walked past her and rang the local police officer in the town some thirty miles away, and asked him to wait at the hospital to see if he could find my duck thief. This officer had been in town a long time. He knew exactly who I was talking about, as a certain person had a reputation for stealing poultry.

My wife and I were having a cup of tea when the phone rang. It was the local police officer. My duck thief had called into the local hospital to have a heap of pellets removed from his posterior. The cop laughed and said that he must have had a good trip to town over the rough stony country road to get to the hospital".

Fathers Handlebar Moustache

My father had a magnificent handle bar mustache when I was a wee lad.

In the morning, before setting off to work, he would reach up to the mantelpiece near the Ansonia Clock and take down a small medicine jar, which was filled with a special wax to treat the hairy appendage on his face. He would wax the ends of the mustache and then twirl the ends as he looked in a small oval mirror. When he was satisfied with the look of it, he would give mum a kiss, then head off to work.

This was a morning ritual, like combing one's hair, washing hands, and cleaning teeth.

One Sunday afternoon after lunch, father had been reading the local paper, then had nodded off to sleep. He was snoring lightly as he snuggled down in the overstuffed chair in front of the fire.

It was bitterly cold outside. I was nursing the cat near the fire; mother had been doing some mending and had gone to the kitchen with one of my sisters to cut up some vegetables to cook with the roast for dinner that night.

Two of the boarders were also sitting in the lounge; both were reading books. Father was snoring, a bit louder now as he was evidently enjoying his nap, after a hard week in the cold, tending the oyster beds near the Kirton Point Jetty.

Billy, one of the boarders, was a bit of a rascal; he was always playing tricks on someone, usually me. Billy looked up from his book, then pointed to mum's mending basket, with all of the scraps of material for mending, needles, wool, cotton, and a large pair of sharp scissors.   I must have looked a bit bemused as he could not get the message across with his sign language. Suddenly I got the meaning of this gestating; He was pointing to his father's lip, then to his mother's scissors, making a chopping motion.

Reaching very carefully for the scissors so as to not wake father, I reached over, and with one quick cut, I sliced one side of his pride and joy, the large mustache. I had cut off about three inches of the mustache, leaving only about a half-inch left on that side

Both of the boarders could hardly stop chuckling softly. They pointed to the missing hair on father's lap.

Father must have been woken by the shenanigans; I was back nursing the cat. Father asked Billy what was so funny, he always liked a good joke, and he thought that he had missed out on one.

Father stretched back in the chair and gave a big yawn; as he did so, he reached for the mustache to give the ends a twirl. A look of horror came across his face. I noticed this and had leaped to my feet. "You, hey you boy. Come here".

I was not that silly; this tone of voice usually meant big trouble. I ran out the door; my father was running after me. I was halfway over the iron fence in the backyard when his boot caught me right up the behind. I went flying over the fence, landing on my back in a huge mud puddle, where Fred, I, and the girls had been damming the water in the vacant block behind our house, to play with making mud pies and castles. Mother came around the end of the fence, calling my name as she did so; she was still laughing. I was hiding a cubby house we had built in a mallee tree. I was freezing cold, muddy, and soaking wet. So I came out and followed her inside the house.

Father was waiting in the Lounge room with his razor strop; He grabbed me and pulled me over his knee. I got two whacks, which hurt even more as my clothes were wet.

As I went to my room to change, I could still hear Billy laughing. I had been set up again by this rotten sod. I was starting to learn, but slowly. Father shaved the remainder of the marvelous mustache off and never attempted to grow one again. I had a few days sitting at school and the meal table on a hard chair with my sore bum.

Another John Henry Ives story, God bless you, John Henry.

Harley in the shed

I had just left school and was lucky to be apprenticed to a plumbing firm that was not too far from our home.

I was very interested in any work that involved using my hands. I found the plumbing business very interesting. Learning to make lead elbows and general pipework, plus digging trenches through the tough limestone, all helped keep me fit.

I was fifteen when I started at Eglington's Plumbing. I was helping with the finances at home by now paying my mother board, and always had enough money left over for going to the movie on Saturday night with my mates and other fishing trips.

The main mode of transport to ferry tools and materials was a nineteen twenty-four Harley Davidson motorbike with a large wooden box on a sidecar. I was fascinated by this machine. It was so big compared to the other motorcycles around town at the time. On occasions, I would sit on the seat of this giant and imagine my driving it down the road to a job.

Some of the workers would tease me about the bike at lunchtime.

I had been working for this firm for six months, and the fascination for this bike did not wane.

Maybe it was the roar of the motor when it was started. I was a bit like a dog wanting to chase cars. One evening at the finish of the day, the Harley was out in the street in front of the shop. One of the men asked me to start the bike and drive it into the shed as they were going to lock up for the night.

This was my big chance. I stood next to the bike and reached over and turned the switch on, and then with an almighty heave for my small frame, gave the kick-started a shove with my foot. The bike started, but unknown to me; it was still in gear; no one had told me about this.

The handlebars pulled out of my hands as the monster roared through the door of the shed, knocking over a new ceramic washbasin as it went. The basin hit the cement floor and smashed into pieces. Then the bike front wheel went through the back wall of the shed, breaking one of the timbers and pushing a sheet of iron off the wall. When the sidecar hit the wall, the bike stalled. All of the guys were laughing their heads off, except for the boss.

The shed was fixed in no time, and luckily the bike appeared to have no damage, but the washbasin that had been smashed took me four weeks to pay for. I was only given enough money to pay mother the board.

They were very long weeks. A lot of my mates teased me about having no money. I really had to stop most of my social activities.

When I finally received my pay packet after the four lean weeks, I looked at the money and went to the boss and told him that he had overpaid me. He explained that the extra money was the money he had kept back each week for the four weeks. He hoped I had learned my lesson well. I sure had after that experience.

John Ives

The Hammer Head Shark

They say one is not too old to learn. Boy, did we have a good learning curve this day?

I had headed down south from Tumby Bay to catch some King George whiting to put in the deep freezer for later in the year; I had a mate with me.

It was Easter Time. This was usually the last time off on a farm for a long time. Getting the farming plant ready for ripping up the seeding and then seeding involved some work. Repairs had to be carried out, Shears changed and any bent or worn parts fixed,

We found a nice patch of Whiting and were putting quite a few big fish into the small icebox on ice. We had also caught some fat garfish and large Tommy Roughs, plus some six squid. One had squirted me in the face when I was landing it into the boat. Black ink dripped off me all over the front of my fishing clothes.

We were about to start the motor and head for home when a four-foot hammerhead shark swam on the surface of the water to the boat. I had never seen one of these before; it was an ugly-looking creature. I had a heavy snapper line ready for a chance snapper sighting in one of the side pockets in the boat. I pulled this out and put a large piece of squid head we had been cutting bait off on the hook. I removed the heavy sinker and then tossed the unweighted line to the shark. He snapped the bait off then went swimming off. I towed hard on the line and had him over the side of the boat on the floor. This was a big mistake. The bloody fish went berserk. It still had the hook in its mouth. The shark turned toward me and pushed its tail against the engine cover and lurched toward me with its mouth snapping; its tail swung violently and smashed a fishing tackle box, sending hooks, floats, and sinkers all over the floor of the boat.

I had no waddy or any other thing to hit this shark with. It was still trying to bite us. A side pocket of the boat filled with hand-lines for fishing was broken off the side of the boat. We were not game to have our feet on the floor. The lines were getting very tangled with the hooks on the floor of the boat. The other side pocket was smashed off by now; this had some fishing rods. The reels and rods were being smashed as the slippery character started to roll. It wound the tangled fishing line around itself.

After nearly an hour, the shark subsided somewhat. We had been sitting with our legs dangling over the side of the now half wrecked boat. I found a long sharp fishing knife on the floor of the boat and drove this through the head of the shark.

The shark shuddered its last moves. I pulled the anchor up into the boat and started the boat motor,

We drove back to Tumby Bay somewhat sorrier but wiser; there was a hell of a mess to clean up the next day.

Monkey business at Coober Pedy

I had been to Coober Pedy for a look with my wife and had stayed a few days with some friends for a bit of a break and a look around. The guy had a small frontend loader and Backhoe. He was working at the Fourteen-mile field and was finding some good opal in the bottom of an old bulldozer cut. We were invited out to have a look at the enterprise.

Reggie had been working with his wife in the area some twenty years before when the big rush was on. He had remembered this cut as it had yielded a lot of opals. Reggie always thought that the cut was not deep enough. He had proved the point and was doing quite well.

There was a big bear of a man working with him who seemed to be a bit slow; he was living next door to Reggie. His name was Black Bart.

Black Bart did not do too much work until some opal was found. The wall of the cut on one side had a thick ironstone-filled fault. The opal ran across the floor of the old cut from this. Reggie had dug down with the backhoe about two meters and was working the face of the new area by drilling and blasting the wall.

We pegged two claims near where Reggie was working.

I would go to Coober Pedy and hire a guy with a drill to look for opal on these claims. Before starting work, I went to check to see if the claims were ok. When I arrived, I noticed that an excavator was tearing into Reggie's claim. I walked over, thinking that Reggie may have bought an excavator, the big bear Black Bart was working with one of the town's crooks. I asked if Reggie still owned the claim; I was told he had left town and was not coming back.

I phoned Reggie that night and asked him about the claim; Reggie was livid, especially when the Black Bart character he had tried to help was one of the crooks. Reggie asked me if I was going to be around for a few days. I said yes. I intended to do about a week's drilling of the claims. Reggie and his wife arrived, I went to see them. Reggie had found out that Black Bart had pulled his mining pegs out and had tossed them down a nearby shaft. Reggie had been out and had re-pegged his claim; the crooks had left. That afternoon I was walking down to the shops with Reg. The crooked town official who owned the excavator was walking toward us. He was shaking hands with all of the Greeks and laughing. He looked up and spied Reg. He tried to pass, Reggie shifted and blocked his way, he attempted again to no avail, and Reggie blocked his way again.

"Hey Eric stop still," warned Reggie; the crook stopped. "I want to ask you something, Eric." Eric thought he had been forgiven, "what do you want to know, " "Why did they make big powerful guns like the 350 Winchesters and the 243 caliber hunting guns" Eric looked a bit bewildered. "I do not know Reggie, why." "They made them shoot claim jumping snakes like you, Eric. Have you ever seen what a 243- caliber rifle does to a kangaroo or a wombat" "No, what, " "It blows their head clean off their shoulders?

One day when you are doing your big man walk and shake all of the hands of the people in the street. Just think I will be lying on one of the shop roofs with a good view of the street. I am going to shoot you. You will not

hear the shot as your head disintegrates into a bloody pulp."

Eric slipped past Reggie and ran as fast as he could down the street. "That will make the mongrel think. He probably thinks I am going to do this. It will keep the crook off the streets for a while". Reggie and I walked back to his house. He had the odd chuckle on the way.

My friend Eric

I first met Eric when a guy I had gone to college with in Adelaide moved next door to us with a noodling machine to look for opal, which had been missed at Coober Pedy.

Bob had been a school prefect when I had boarded at Prince Alfred College. He had a reputation for being a smartarse. At any excuse, he would front the student and tell those to come to his room that night. Bob shared a room with another prefect. Bob would have the lad bend over his bed; he would take his slipper and put a cake of soap in it, then give the lad six hits on the bum as hard as he could.

We were digging some opal we had found with the old bulldozer when we noticed the group of men standing on the top of our bulldozer cut. I recognized Bob; he had not changed much, still looked like a smart-ass

I invited the men to come down into the cut to have a look. Bob had his father and a couple of mates and a distinguished-looking man who looked about seventy years old. Bob introduced all of the men. I took notice of Eric, Bob's ex-father-in-law.

I spent some time talking to Eric that day and could not help notice that he displayed an air of intelligence that his Ex son in law severely lacked.

The next time I met Eric, I was at Coober Pedy fixing the Bulldozer. We had the motor out of the monster and had it in a shed in pieces. I met him in the street without his partner. We had a good talk about interesting things.

I was invited to a Lions Meeting by an Irishman who dealt in opals. Eric was at this meeting. Eric had a real presence about him. On Sunday, instead of sitting in the dugout watching the box, I decided to go to church at the Catacomb Underground Church; Eric was there, I sat next to him.

After the church meeting, I asked Eric to have dinner with me. I had made a stew and had a mistake; I thought I was putting some relish into the chicken leg stew but had realized it was apricot jam. This was a very good mistake as it was really tasty. This started our friendship. I would pick up Eric, who had lost his license, and take him to church and then to dinner.

Eric had been an airline pilot, starting in the nineteen-thirties. He started his career flying Dragon Rapide's, a cloth-covered twin-engine bi-plane. He flew to Port Lincoln with Guinea Airways; during his years at Guinea Airways, he had graduated from the Dragon to Lockheed six's which carried six passengers to Lockheed Eight, then to Lockheed Electra's a ten-passenger plane.

Eric then told me he had met the love of his life when the Douglas DC three had come available.

Eric told me that he was ninety-two years old. I did not really believe him. He had lost his license some two years before when he had some problems with his memory and health. His wife had died many years before. He had the daughter who had been married to the smart ass,

When he had lost his license, he was feeling lost; one of the lion's members had seen a DC 3 plane land at the Coober Pedy airport. They thought Eric would like to go and see the plane. Two guys picked him up and drove him to the airport. Eric had clambered up the steps into the plane, where he met a guy who was a junior pilot when he was retiring from TAA airlines, where he had been flying Douglas DC6B's and Lockheed Super Constellations all over the World. He had invited Eric to sit in the pilot's seat. He had spent many hours sitting in this seat during the war when he was a civilian lieutenant in the Air Force. He had started the motor and was taxiing the large plane back and forth along the Coober Pedy runway while waiting for the tourists to return from town. I asked what he really wanted to do; Ï wanted to give her some revs and pull the stick back, "He replied.

Eric was always looking to get himself a new woman. Even at the age of ninety-four, this was Eric's main aim in life. I commented one day about how he already had a lady friend, a local widow, Bev.

He commented on how Bev was not interested in intimate relations. I laughed; Eric was adamant he was looking for more than friendship.

I smiled at Eric and said. "Eric, aren't you a bit worried that the powder might have gotten a bit damp over the years and the gun might not work anymore." Eric looked at me in a very serious matter and said the gun was still in extremely good order, even after the lack of use. He had no worries in that department. I thought at the time I would like to know his secret for when I get older

Caught down a mine shaft

Rob, his wife, and two kids had traveled to Andamooka opal fields to try to augment some extra money to back up the small farm. Wool and sheep prices were very poor at the time.

They had found an abandoned shack and moved in with some scant furniture and an old kerosene refrigerator, and a small portable gas stove. The shack had a small rainwater tank that had to be refilled from a well and tank many miles away if there was no rain to fill it. The water was ferried back in forty-four-gallon drums in the rear of his old Austin A forty ute. The water was then pumped out by hand into the tank.

The weather was hot; the unlined corrugated iron walls did not help. Rob had worked for months with his mate without finding opal. They both were extremely short of money.

The shaft dirt and rock after blasting was mucked out with a Yorke Hoist. The hoist consisted of a steel pole set into the ground next to a shaft. A motorized hoist was attached to the pole, which worked by friction wheels and handles. When the handle was pulled up, the wheels met with the pulley set up on the motor, which lifted the heavy bucket out of the shaft. The bucket was then swung away from the entrance to the shaft, then lowered to the ground, and then the dirt was tipped from the drum. The buckets were filled at the face of the drive then wheeled with a modified wheelbarrow to the shaft to be lifted up end out. This machine was a far cry from the hand-wound windlass used previously.

Rob and his mate had been to the railway line some miles away to get old discarded railway sleepers to put around the top of the shaft as the dirt had built up.

The men had finally found a seam of good-paying opal. They were elated about this but kept their mouths tightly shut about this as there had been an influx of some Serbian and Croatian men starting to mine in this area. These men had no scruples and would have robbed the pennies off a dead man's eyes.

Rob and Gerry had gone to work one morning and had found that someone had been digging in the face of the drive where they had finally found the opal

This claim was close to town. After the robbery, Rob would go to check the claim every night. He would drive his old utility out toward the claim then walk to the shaft with a small flashlight.

After six nights, he looked down the shaft and saw a torchlight being flashed around. Rob then carefully put four sleepers over the top of the shaft; he then ran back to the utility. He drove back to the claim and then drove the utility on top of the sleepers.

Rob walked the mile home and had told his wife about the trapped man. Late the next day, he went to the police station and told them about the man in the shaft. The officer said that they were going to be busy the next day. He would come out to the claim just before dark.

Two police officers waited as Rob took the utility off the sleepers. The cops had to help push it back. The sleepers were removed, and a distraught-looking man climbed out into the dying sunlight. He went with the police.

The man was told to leave town and not to come back; He knew what some of the other miners would do to him as the word had gotten out about the robbery; Justice was sometimes quite brutal in these small communities when a thief or pedophile had been found.

The thief quickly tossed his possessions together and left town. The next morning Rob was leaving his home. As he undid the door, he noticed a plug of gelignite stuck to the door with a short fuse and detonator in it. A note was written on a small piece of paper 'next time we light fuse'. There was one less crook in town, who evidently had some mates.

A Successful Turkey Shoot

I have heard a story of some people going out into the Opal field one Sunday trying to shoot a rabbit or a Bush Turkey,

The family packed a barbeque and took some sausages and mutton chops. They went past the Fifteen-mile field and drove through the stunted bushes, then down off the plateau to an interesting hollow surrounded by hills.

The kids collected some twigs and other wood to fire up the Barbie; when the meat was cooked, the family ate the chops and sausages with a slice of bread with tomato sauce. Mum and dad settled down with a bottle or two of Southwark beer. The kids took off and played in the sand, and chased each other through the bushes.

After a couple of hours, their mum yelled out for them to come and get in the car; they were ready to go home. The kids piled into the car. Bert let the clutch out; the car sank down in the rear; they were bogged in the soft dirt.

Bert and the kids were trying to push the car out. Bert had a shovel in the boot. He started to dig the car out; one of the kids rushed into the pile of dirt and retrieved a large piece of good opal. The car was a minor concern then. They loaded the boot of the car with good opal then drove back to town. The car had plenty of room to drive out of the boggy sand by then. The next day the father and mother went and pegged claims on the spot. That is how the Seventeen Mile field was discovered.

Cat and dog droppings

"Come out and have a look. The dirty sods have been at it again" Jean came to the front door and peered out at the mess on the veranda. "What do you think we can do to get rid of them?". There were yellow pools of cat urine on the shiny red cement veranda floor. "If I were game, I would find the .22 rifle and shoot the dirty sods ". I knew that this was out of the question as we were in a highly built-up part of town.

The cat urine and dog poo were an ongoing problem; I had tried all of the old wife's tale recipes like cloudy ammonia and garlic to no avail. The nightly ritual of laying one's claim to the territory of the veranda and the fights and fur plus the yellow pools of urine were getting far beyond a joke.

When at the shops the next morning, I spied some firecrackers in a box. I bought a pack of ten medium-sized crackers.

" This will do the trick," I thought.

I set about making myself a slingshot like we used to have when we were kids. I was pretty pleased with the results.

The next night I was ready and armed with my new invention. The din started as the rowdy cats started to hiss and growl.

I opened the front door, and they shot off the veranda and started to fight on the lawn about five meters away. I placed the firecracker in the pouch of the slingshot and lit the fuse, then quickly grabbed the handle and fired the missile at the cats. The firecracker exploded just above their heads; with a loud screech, the offending cats ran off down the road. I had my first win.

We also had the problem of wandering dogs using our lawn for a place to drop their poo at night. The following night, I let one of the dogs have the same explosive treatment. He did not like the experience either.

Two nights later, I had my nemesis; the tom cat's back; I was on the veranda and had just lit the fuse of the cracker and had grabbed the handle and was drawing the rubber back when the cracker exploded in my hand. It hurt like hell. I went back inside and bathed my hand in Dettol and hot water for a while to relieve the pain. The blasted cats had definitely won that round

Around nine in the morning, I had an unwelcome visitor. A Police car drove into my driveway. The officer came to the door. "I have a complaint that you have been firing a gun at night; one of the neighbors is worried about this. "I explained to the officer what I had been using to try to get rid of my cat and dog problem. "Nothing seems to be working. The bloody cracker went off in my hand last night and nearly blew my finger off". I showed him my mangled thumb. The cop thought for a while, " May-be you need an electric fence to give them a boot." I had not thought of this idea before. "Thanks, mate. I will give your idea a try". The officer was laughing as he went to his car.

I asked around and found a farmer mate who had a small portable electric fence charger he was not using.

I spent the rest of the day setting the wire across the two gates into the circular driveway and just inside the fence along with the lawn. This should catch any cat which jumped over the fence.

That night before I went to bed, I turned the fencer on and checked to see if it was working with an insulated screwdriver. A loud crack, then a bright spark jumped across the wires.

During the night, we heard a dog screaming and yelping as it were the first victim; a short time later, the was another loud woofing and yelping as the offending dog left in a hurry. It was now the cat's command performance; about six of them got the treatment. A short time later, there was a huge commotion and the sound of broken glass; I had forgotten about the milkman delivering the milk during the night. He had some really nasty things to say about me at this time.

I waited up the next night until three am with a bottle of port wine as a sorry gift. The milky had a bit of a laugh about the experience. He was not laughing the night before.

The dogs and cats had at least got the message. I would string the wire across the drive and then take it down about midnight for a few nights.

A Huge Whale Shark

During the summer school holidays, my mates and I spent many hours on both the Kirton Point and Brennan's Jetty. We either just fished for mainly sweet Tommy Roughs, Garfish, or Salmon Trout.

We were very interested in watching the bagged grain being loaded onto the large wind jammers which carried the grain back to Europe and England. We Knew a lot of the Wharfie's who worked there. A couple of mates' fathers did this job.

Occasionally some of the crew of the ships would board at our boarding house if there was room. I think they were happy to be able to leave the tough conditions on the ship while in port. I remember well the funny accents some of the men had. Some had eyes for my sisters. They took joy in teasing these men in jest.

When the ships were seen on the horizon, they would sail to an area known as the ballast grounds; here, they would unload the sand and rocks used as ballast to keep the ships upright as they sailed to Australia.

When the job was finished, they would raise the sails again to sail to the wharf in Port Lincoln.

The Pilot Launch a twenty-five-foot cutter would be driven out and wait for the ships to sail closer to the wharf. When they were not far out, the launch would steam up to the sailing ship and transfer a Pilot aboard to guide the ship through the channels to the wharf.

I was asked if I would like to take a ride out to wait for the ship one day. The boat usually found a good fishing spot, where the Pilot and skipper would drop their lines and catch some nice fish. I was into the fishing part, plus I was interested to see how the Pilot was transferred to the sailing ship.

The day was not very windy, so the windjammer was taking its time getting to us. We had caught a nice lot of fish.

The skipper of the boat looked over the side and yelled. "Have a look in the water below the boat. There is the biggest shark I have ever seen." We all looked at this monster. It was a darkish green color with rows of yellow spots in lines along its body.

I ran to the bow of the boat. There were at least six feet poking out the front; I then ran to the stern and noticed that the shark also was out from the stern by four feet. We estimated that the shark was nearly forty feet long. It was just lying still sheltering under our boat. The two men on board had never seen or had been told of anything like this before.

We were not too sure what the shark was going to do, so the Pilot pulled the anchor, while the skipper started the motor. We steamed toward the approaching windjammer and offloaded the Pilot to the wooden and rope ladder. The sea monster was left behind.

I hope you enjoyed these tales of the ocean and the tales of the land.

These stories are usually lost and can never be found again

Thank You

The End

ooooo OOOOOO ooooo

www.ingramcontent.com/pod-product-compliance
Lightning Source LLC
Chambersburg PA
CBHW071929290426
44110CB00013B/1534